TESTIMONIALS

"As a spokesperson for the animals Stephanie's book provides us with an open, honest, insightful and informative guide to Holistic Grooming. This delightful, easy to read book gives examples (which we can all relate to) and throughout, Stephanie's knowledge, love, respect and dedication for our four-legged friends wholeheartedly shines through. This book is suitable not only for those working in the industry, but for all animal guardians too. With the help of this book, I hope that trust and the strongest of bonds will be formed through mutual understanding."

Joanne Jarvis. Author of Dexter's Diary. Holistic Therapist and Animal Communicator.

THE MAGIC OF HOLISTIC GROOMING

A NO-NONSENSE GUIDE ON HOW TO PAWSITIVELY GROOM YOUR DOG WITH LESS STRESS

STEPHANIE ZIKMANN

Carmela,

It was so lovely to chat with you! Enjoy the book ♡

Love,

Stephanie

xxx

Foreword by
DR. ISLA FISHBURN

authors
AND CO.

CONTENTS

"Common Sense maintains the status quo, so we continue to do what we know best, rather than seeking out the best that we can do."

— DR. SUSAN FRIEMAN

trainers to walkers to groomers as it provides a full and detailed picture of what is expected of a groomer and what are the best practices they should be considering if not following. Its also a great book for dog owners too, it clearly shows what you should be considering before choosing a groomer and how to find the groomer who is best for their dog.
This book is easy to read, I love the conversational tone and Stephanie really takes you on the journey with her.
High recommend this book for everyone.

Suzanne Gould aka The Rescue Dog Ranger, Edinburgh Holistic Dogs.
www.edinburghholisticdogs.co.uk

GIVING THANKS

Jo Watson – for the amazing editing skills that make the book as fluent, and perfect (in my eyes) as it could possibly have been. www.agoodwriteup.com. Oh my Fluff! Where would I be without you.

Esme Kira Illustrations – for the book cover illustration, and the other quirky features throughout the book that give it the character it deserves. www.scruffylittleherbert.com

Nicole Zikmann – my little sis, who spent an entire afternoon snapping my launch photo's in preparation for the release of this book – you did a wonderful job!

Abi, and her team at Authors & Co – for the guidance, support, and hard-work you and your team have put in throughout the creation of the book, and for making this experience so memorable. www.authorsandco.pub

To my Beta Readers and Fellow Pet Professionals – Joanne Jarvis, Suzanne Gould, Alex Smith, Ally Waidson, Lisa Willcox, Si Jones, Tracey Rose, Kristen Finely, Sophie Badger, Silvia Caminiti King, Lizi Arnold, Lindsey-Marie Taylor, Sue Williamson, and Emma Steadman - thank you for brainstorming with me in the early days, and for keeping it real.

To my Mentors and Teachers – Helen Motteram, Dr. Isla Fishburn, and Rachel Spencer. Without the constant wisdom, advice and guidance (especially when things got particularly tough), I wouldn't have had the guts to keep going.

DEDICATION

I would never have been able to fulfil this childhood dream without the support, love, and constant cheerleading of my husband, Scott and our two boys Jack and Joey. You are the reason I continue to push myself each day, and I hope this book makes you proud.

And to my four furry companions at home, who continually share their human with all of her doggie clients at work. Even though you can smell other dogs from my work clothes, you still welcome me home with tail wags, and wet kisses. Jessica, King Louis, Nala and Lola – thank you for your daily teachings.

Lastly, to all of my clients (past and present) at my spa, Scrub A Dug Dug – Canine Spa & Boutique, and their beloved canines – without you, I wouldn't be the groomer I am today.

I love you all.

DISCLAIMER

The accuracy of the quotes used within this book, and their attribution has been checked, where possible, however in some instances the source is anonymous, or unknown. If the makers of these quotes have been inaccurately presented, or misattributed we ask that they would kindly notify the author, so that she may take the reasonable steps to correct this on any reprinting.

For ease of reading, the author refers to the animal in the masculine unless in specific case studies, additionally where the term "handler" is used this refers to any person responsible for the care of the animal whether that is guardian, groomer or other professional.

All personal information has been changed accordingly for use in all featured Case Studies to comply with the Data Protection Act 2018, and GDPR.

FOREWORD

Several years ago now, I was visiting an animal teaching college for the possibility of delivering some lessons to the students. As I was shown around the college, I was taken to a training room where students were learning and practicing within a grooming "environment". When I entered the room, I felt a sudden rush of panic, shock and disbelief about this training environment where both young and inexperienced students, as well as dogs, were placed. It was chaos.

My initial thoughts were, "what is this teaching the students about what is acceptable? And how is this experience affecting the dog?" There were rows of grooming tables, noise, dogs being shouted at, dogs being made to stand and to stop "being naughty," dogs looking miserable, stressed, terrified and not one person seemed to bat an eyelid at the intensity of it all. "Is it just me thinking this entire set up is all wrong?" I thought to myself. I did just that - kept my thoughts to myself as I was taken into another room.

Here, the dogs were kept in a kennel area waiting to be groomed. "Phew," I thought as I took a deep breath of relief to be out of the grooming room. My thoughts were still very much in there though, and I was genuinely shocked by the little to no consideration for the dog being groomed, who, after all, was supposed to be having a grooming experience. I was still focused on "what on earth is this teaching the young students?"

Just when I didn't think it could get any worse, it did! I think what I was failing to express verbally was evidently seen in my face. A kennel door was opened and a beautiful black Newfoundland happily bounced out and was led to the door that opened to the main grooming room. Hearing, and I am certain also sensing, the chaos and panic that he was about to meet, the dog stopped and began to pull backwards in panic. It was clear that the dog was unhappy and scared. The teacher and two students were able to get hold of the dog. I wasn't worried, recognising his fear, or assuming they had recognised it, I was expecting them to find a way to make the dog be more comfortable. You know, perhaps a place where he could be groomed on his own, perhaps abandoning the groom altogether, perhaps waiting until there was less dogs and less noise. I was expecting SOMETHING...but I wasn't expecting what actually happened.

Grabbing hold of the dog, two of them held him by his neck as they pulled him into the room whilst the other pushed him from behind. This poor dog was dragged into a room that he was clearly expressing he had a reluctance and fear of. I was so taken aback that I didn't quite know what to say to the person showing me around. Again, no one seemed to bat an eyelid or question how this may affect the dog for the rest of its life. Yes, I do mean the rest of its life – how that one experience could have the potential to affect the rest of that dog's life, not just towards being groomed but a whole host of other situations; kennels, young females, adult females, going to strange places, having its lead put on, being touched, smelling a smell similar to a smell from that day, hearing a noise similar to a noise from that day...the list goes on. I thought to myself, "is there no consideration for how all of this is having an affect on the dog and what they are learning from this?"

Still, I kept quiet, being the polite potential teaching candidate I was. Yet, what I observed plagued me throughout my journey home and for the rest of the day. It still plagued me days after and I certainly developed a different idea to what I previously had thought about grooming schools and teaching environments. There was no concept about canine behaviour and understanding for how the experience might be for a dog. Before you ask, I declined the teaching post.

A few years later, I was asked by a grooming school to give a weekend seminar to a group of groomers so that they could learn more about canine behaviour, language and how to support the dogs that came into their own grooming salon. I was a little nervous at first; would they hate me for what I would share and not like what I had to say? Would they even care? Would they argue with the considerations I was going to state that a dog needed? Would they be as interested in behaviour and supporting a dog as much as I was and want everyone in the dog sector to be?

The experience at the grooming college had really impacted my thoughts on where a groomer's focus may be – that day at the college it was evident that it wasn't the dog. I didn't want this experience to cloud my judgement and speaking to an independent grooming school would give me that chance to meet other groomers who were qualified and experienced.

What a breath of fresh air they were!

There was much shared that day and I always remember one thing that the groomers shared with me. When I spoke with them about the challenges that could arise with handling a dog's feet, it being an area that, to a dog, signifies their fitness and survival (think of it like someone tying your hands behind your back and you feeling ok about that), they shared with me that it is the feet they are taught to groom first. I am not sure if this has since changed in grooming schools, but I remember that always stuck out to me. Knowing what I know about canines, the feet would certainly not be the first area I would groom on a dog, certainly a dog that did not know me.

As we chatted in the lunch break, I learned more about what is expected of groomers and the dogs being groomed, as well as their genuine care for the dog to have the best experience possible. In fact, I developed some long-standing friendships with some of the groomers and I know of several that frequently remind me and share with others how my teachings have dramatically changed how they operate their own grooming salon. That is always so humbling for me to know.

Being a groomer is not easy. I don't think I could do it and I take my hat off to each one of you. Being a groomer that truly wants to operate as a Holistic Groomer is harder still, but it is achievable. I personally know a few groomers that operate this way and I admire them for it. Their desire to do all they can to improve the grooming environment, make it that touch better in some way or learn about a new product, technique or practice that can improve their grooming style or comfort for the dog whilst in their care is admirable. Not only do groomers have to keep up do date with new equipment, training for different breed and breed styling and various CPD, but they also have to be cleaner, receptionist, behaviourist, dog handler and the voice of reason to unreasonable clients who are unfairly disapproving of their dog's groom, even though they can't even wipe a tear from their own dog's eye. Yes, being a groomer is a profession based and built on passion with the desire to do a good service for the dog. Just somewhere, for some groomers the focus has become distorted.

I admire my friends who I would consider to be Holistic Groomers for their commitment and I admire everyone working in this industry that are playing their part in making, learning, exploring and creating change in a dog's grooming experience; everything from salon set up, products used and, of course, consideration for the dog itself and how s/he is feeling in a grooming environment. There was a time when a statement, such as, "just make the dog do it" was accepted and I am delighted that more and more in the canine profession are moving in to more conscious awareness of compassion, relationship, compromise and consideration for our canine friends

– a truly heart led approach, which is where all animals live and respond from (including humans!). To me, it is about a relationship where we have an understanding of how another feels.

This is why I admire and am cheering Stephanie on with her commitment and search for how she can not only improve the grooming environment for dogs, but also improve the grooming environment for you, the groomer; those of you who show up every day with a focus on wanting to be better, do better and know better than what you did yesterday. It is a huge commitment you have agreed to take on for the sake of a dog that belongs to another. So, be proud of yourself – I am proud of you.

For a long time now I have hoped for a book like the Magic of Holistic Grooming to be available to all groomers and I am so in awe of Stephanie for creating such a book that is, indeed, magical! There is so much in this book for a groomer that goes beyond what you are probably expecting. Stephanie has every base covered, even those bases that you didn't even know existed or thought of!

Stephanie is committed to making a difference and this is evident in The Magic of Holistic Grooming. It is filled with love, compassion, authenticity and vulnerability as she writes from the heart on every page and shares personal experiences of her grooming background, the concerns, the back-lash, the judgement, the fear, the criticism and how, regardless, she carried on with her purpose – to be a voice and make a change for both groomers and dogs in your care. It takes deep trust and bravery to speak up when something does not feel right, when a change is being suggested and when you question something that has been the norm for so long on an industry level.

This book is beautifully written, not from a place of judgement or blame but from truth, honesty and personal experience of Stephanie's struggles, successes, stories and journey to her constantly evolving practice as a holistic dog groomer. Here, she shares it all with you so that you, too, can begin or expand on your own journey into Holistic Grooming. The dogs you see, their human guardians, your family, your friends, the industry itself and yourself will thank you for it.

- Dr Isla Fishburn
Founder of Kachina Canine and Sacred Creator
Canine Wellness Advisor, Behaviourist and Shamanic
Practitioner

1

THE PHILOSOPHY OF HOLISTIC GROOMING

"Do what you love and you will never have to work a day in your life."

— CONFUCIUS

THIS BOOK HAS BEEN CAREFULLY STRUCTURED TO TAKE readers through a very specific journey in Holistic Grooming, therefore the chapters ahead should be read in the order they are presented.[1]

But remember that Holistic Grooming is not just the dabbling of non-conventional therapies, or using natural products – I wanted to delve deeper into the purpose of "holism", and why it's important for us all to embrace a far broader perspective when working in an industry that relies so much on *quality* of care.

Let's begin with some of my most frequently asked questions…

What is 'Holistic Grooming'?

Holistic Grooming isn't just about preening the dog in front of you and achieving perfect symmetry and style. Holistic Grooming is about how we can enhance overall health and wellbeing through the benefits of grooming itself.

Holistic Grooming is a practice that every groomer and guardian should embrace. Who doesn't want to feel more connected to themselves, and their dog? Who doesn't want to learn ways to make grooming a less stressful experience? Who doesn't want to learn how to adapt their approach to get better results?

If you're looking to enhance your experience in the grooming environment, build your business and skillset on solid foundations, and promote resilience in dogs, you can start that embracing right now, right here in this book.

Still with me?

So, some people may call me a 'liberal' or a 'snowflake' (whatever that even means), because maybe what I'm about to write in this book is far-fetched, completely bonkers, and a 'woo woo' waste of your money, but I know that *for me*, Holistic Grooming has massively improved the health and wellbeing of all of the dogs that have padded in through my doors, and that's what makes it all worthwhile for me as a professional groomer and a lover of animals.

I want you to at least try it. Or humour me, perhaps. I know this book can help you.

Whether you have 20 years of dog grooming experience behind you, or you're only just starting out, it really doesn't matter. Anyone can - and everyone *should* - learn Holistic Grooming.

So, for the rest of this book, let's drop the labels (my name's Stephanie, by the way) and make a promise to one another to hold off on judgment - at least until the last page has been turned (or you've chucked it in the bin).

What Is The Purpose Of Holistic Grooming?

The purpose of everything this book wants and needs to share with you will not only improve the health and wellbeing of both yourself and the dogs you groom, but it will make for a more relaxing experience in your work. And who doesn't want that in the workplace?

Whilst it's never going to be realistic to remove stress completely from the grooming experience, it is immensely healthy and achievable to reduce the amount of stress that is often experienced amongst dogs, groomers and guardians when it's carried out the 'traditional' way.

Holistic Grooming is about being mindful of the consequences of our actions, and how our environment interacts and communicates with us on a cellular, energetic, physical, physiological and spiritual level.

It sounds complex, and I'm not going to lie - it *can* be.

But when we niche it right down to the specific grooming environment we already work in, it really doesn't need to be any more complex than grooming already is for us. And the beauty is that once you know how Holistic Grooming can make a difference, it will all start to make perfect sense.

What Does 'Holistic' Mean?

Pick your favourite dictionary. For ease, I'm using Dictionary.com, where the term 'holistic' has two adjective (descriptive) meanings, which are:

1. Incorporating the concept of holism, or the idea that the whole is more than merely the sum of its parts - in theory or in practice (holistic psychology).
2. Identifying with principles of holism in a system of therapeutic principles, especially ones considered outside the mainstream of scientific medicine, as naturopathy, or chiropractic, and often involving nutritional measures (holistic medicine).

But what about the phrase, 'Holistic Grooming'? What does that entail? And yes, that was a pun...

Holistic Grooming is considering our entire service based on its entire context, including:

- History and Evolution
- Location and Environment
- Genetics and Heritage
- Lifestyle and Health

- Approach and Handling
- Observation and Communication
- Equipment and Products
- Working Relationships and Synchronised Care
- Compassion and Self-Care
- Empathy and The Forever Student

Phew!

If you can learn how to think outside the box and see the grooming process and environment through the eyes of your *dog*, then you are already halfway there!

ACTIVITY

I want you to pretend you're back at school for a minute. Ah, the joys of acne, unruly hair, and train-track braces... Just me? Moving on...

Okay, so you're back at school, and you're in your English/Drama class. Your teacher calls on you to play the role of Bruno, the scaredy-cat dog. Pretend it's for an upcoming show or something.

Bruno's Bio: Bruno is literally afraid of his own shadow (he just doesn't understand why it keeps following him!)

As you get into character, you realise that life for Bruno is pretty stressful. He is tense all the time. He is jumpy, he is anxious, he is stressed, he doesn't sleep well, he can't relax, and every noise and sudden movement is a trigger.

You have some fun in the role, sure. But would you like to play this character every day for the rest of your life?

Learning to put yourself in your dog's paws will give you an invaluable insight into the life they lead, especially when it comes to the grooming environment. There are so many factors, influences and emotions to consider in that situation.

As a groomer, you really need to get to know as much about the dog in front of you as you can, and have an idea of how you are going to approach the grooming session ahead. There are six things to consider in the first instance:

- **Genetics** – How well-bred is Bruno? Was it a reputable breeder? Are there any hereditary illnesses?
- **Background** – Who is Bruno? What makes him tick? How well has he been socialised? What is his health like? Does he have any allergies? Do the guardians have any allergies? Does he have any particular phobias? Have there been any significant events in his life? What makes Bruno the individual that he is? Is he reactive to anything?
- **Lifestyle** – What does Bruno's routine look like? Where does he sleep? Does he have a 'safe space'? When is he fed? What is he fed? What is his guardian(s) like? Who else lives at home? How old are they? Are there any members of the family who have poor health? Does he have a dog walker, behaviourist and/or trainer? How do they operate?
- **Location** – Where does he stay? Is it rural, or urban? Where is your salon located? Is there parking? Is it busy? Is it near a busy road? Do you have outdoor access? Is it walking distance for Bruno? Is it ground floor? Have you got neighbours?
- **Environment** – How do you operate your business (multi, mobile, one-to-one)? How noisy is it? How busy is it? How well does everything inside the salon flow? Are there any unnecessary objects and/or obstructions? Are you walk-in or appointment only? What's the security and safety like? What flooring do you have? What lighting? How does the space smell? What cleaning products do you use?
- **Approach** – Do you know how to handle Bruno? Do

you know how to use our body language to communicate with him safely? Can you cater to his individual needs? Does he require a more experienced groomer?

I know, there's a lot to consider when thinking about grooming Bruno, isn't there? But try not to get put off just yet…

Holistic Grooming Changes Our Perspective

When we talk about coming from a 'holistic place', we really mean we are looking at the ENTIRE situation, and not just an individual part.

So, if a dog bites you, he isn't 'bad' – though he may be labelled so.

Think about what's really going on here.

Why is this dog biting in the first place?

What can you do to handle (not control – there's a big difference) the dog?

I guess what I'm saying is that we need to delve into the mechanics of what's going on *behind* the bite.

I'm looking under the surface where the suppressed emotion is lying and I'm asking myself:

What is the cause of this dog's behaviour?

What makes this dog tick?

What happened in the moments prior to the bite?

The Importance Of The Holistic Grooming Approach

Case Study

Teddy the Pomeranian has to be the devil incarnate. He'll take your face off the minute you fail to strap him up like a Hannibal Lector stunt double when launched into social situations.

He always has this crazy look in his eye that makes Johnny from The Shining look perfectly attuned, and despite exhausting every known handling restraint there is, he still manages to crocodile roll around the grooming table in a blind rage every time he's booked in for a spruce.

This dog has issues. And you? You can't risk losing a finger, and so, you decide to black-list him.

Now, this is a massive shame for Teddy, really. We don't want to have to deprive any animal of grooming – and you'll find out why, later in the book.

Rather than affirming that "*Teddy is aggressive*", or referring him on to the next groomer brave (or dumb) enough to accept him, ask yourself:

What if nobody wants to groom Teddy? What happens to him then?

The chances are, you've started reading this book because you've tried to handle a difficult dog in the past and would quite like to learn how to handle a difficult dog in the future. Let's build your confidence and begin changing lives like Teddy's for the better then, shall we?

ACTIVITY

Repeat After Me:

1. **There is no such thing as a bad dog – just a bad situation.**
2. **There is no such thing as a dog that can't be helped – just a person not confident enough to do the helping.**
3. **There is bad experience and there is good experience – it's all about knowing the difference between the two.**

Labelling our animals (and ourselves) can be really restrictive and will set us up for an abundance of failures if we are not careful.

Don't get into the habit of letting stereotypes obstruct your passion to excel and grow, but instead allow the holistic approach to open your mind, and unlock doors to many opportunities that will set you up for life-changing success.

Holistic Grooming changes lives for the better, it really does.

Holistic Grooming Is About Safe-Handling

I mentioned that there is a difference between handling and control, and that's true.

Holistic Groomers are encouraged to develop their actual, physical handling skills rather than relying solely on handling aids. This is because dogs require an element of freedom and choice to feel safe.

In later Chapters we will talk more about why it's often safer, and more efficient, to use fewer restraints when working with anxious and/or fearful dogs, but for now let's try and make a mental note that safe-handling is more about how we communicate with a dog, and handle them with our body, and hands.

Holistic Grooming Incorporates Positive Training Techniques And Methods

Additionally, there is only one thing we must remember in regards to training a dog in the grooming environment:

Positive Reinforcement wins every time. That means we will add something positive to encourage a desired behaviour, and never (ever) use punishment.

Holistic Groomers are all about positive training methods, meaning that punishment (in whatever form) is strictly unacceptable. This includes (but is not limited to) corrector sprays, raised voices, and smacking.

. . .

Why Is Holistic Grooming So Successful?

I'm glad you asked!

- It enhances the bond between handler and the dog.
- It develops the groomer's understanding and confidence in doing their job well, thus increasing their productivity and success in their role.
- It gets to the *cause* of behaviours, therefore enabling the groomer to resolve many of the dog's and the guardian's most common problems (fear, anxiety, pain, and stress).
- It reduces the likelihood of burnout in the groomer - and sensory overload in the dog.
- It instils confidence in the dog, groomer and guardian.
- It builds the dog's resilience for future situations.
- It brings additional value and unique selling points to the groomer's business.

And the list goes on.

When we see things from a more wholesome perspective, we can develop our compassion and empathy towards ourselves and others more successfully. This insight enables us to devise creative ways to adapt our entire approach to suit a dog's individual needs.

Additionally, our relationship with ourselves is also nurtured, but we will talk more on that later.

. . .

How Do We Learn Holistic Grooming?

1. Read this book. Yep – I'm biased.
2. Enrol on the Accredited Holistic Grooming Diploma via The Holistic Grooming Academy.
3. Further invest in your education and training, and continue to do so for the rest of your working life (exclusive discounts to webinars, events and courses that I recommend can also be found at the back of this book under 'Resources' – you're welcome!)
4. Finally, allow yourself to believe in a little bit of magic, because a lot about Holistic Grooming *is* truly magical.

ACTIVITY

Repeat After Me:

I promise to open my mind to the information in this book without becoming defensive. No judgements, no name-calling.

Eradicating Myths About Holistic Grooming

Let me set the record straight on a few things about Holistic Grooming:

- There is no such thing as a cookie-cutter approach. All animals require a bespoke approach to their grooming - no ifs or buts! (Butts are for sniffing and pooping, silly).
- Holistic Grooming isn't a sales gimmick, or a niche to

try and blow competitors out of the water. It's a genuine and sincere practice that all pets and their handlers deserve to benefit from.

- There's no such thing as 'perfection', or an 'expert' that knows it all (we are all trying our best and simply learning as we grow).

What Am I Going To Learn Through Holistic Grooming?

Here's the pawesome part:

Holistic Grooming begins to show you how to achieve many things, including:

- How to read an animal's body language (including that of our own!).
- How to listen to our intuition (because they say it's *usually* right).
- How to see things from another being's perspective (because compassion is everything).
- How to be more connected to ourselves and to others (cue the Lion King quote, *"We are one"*).
- How to recognise and manage stress in a positive way (this is called self-love by the way).
- How to safely handle an animal (understanding why less is often more).
- How to employ positive training techniques (to build solid foundations based on trust).
- How to feel good about your work (because good ethics make you feel as warm and fuzzy as a freshly preened Pomski).

- How to run a successful business (because at the end of the day, we all want to make money doing something we are PROUD of).

And so much more!

Holistic Grooming is INVALUABLE

I'm not the only 'crazy' person who believes that the holistic approach to grooming actually works, by the way. Science backs it, too.

Not only that, there are many amazing and wonderful pet professionals who are already advocating for a more holistic approach to all pet care sectors. Allow me to give thanks to some of our friends, teachers, colleagues, and supporters:

Dr. Isla Fishburn, Alison McKinnon, Joanne Jarvis, Rachel Jackson, Lisa Tenzin-Dolma, June Pennell, Caroline Griffiths, Caroline Wilkinson, Jennifer Dow, Mary Burgess, Andrew Hale, Sarah Fisher, Freya Locke, Ruby Leslie, Helen Motteram, Helen Leach, and Sue Williamson (I've probably missed someone, but you know who you are if I have - sorry!).

What's all the more interesting is that during the research for this book, I came across an inspiring grooming manual, 'Holistic Pet Grooming' by Daryl Conner and Mary Oquendo, which highlighted to me that Holistic Grooming isn't such a new concept after-all. And while I had every intention of covering many of the topics Mary and Daryl wrote about (specifically alternative therapies), I decided to instead provide fresh information in areas of Holistic Grooming that hadn't yet been covered in any grooming manuals thus far (if that's not accurate and I've missed the memo, then I do apologise!). I hope you don't mind the last-minute change of plans!

Moving on!

Can Anyone Be A Holistic Groomer?

First remember that Holistic Grooming is the practice of life-long learning and not necessarily a one-off course that we can take, pass, and print a certificate for.

Someone asked me recently how to "qualify" as a Holistic Groomer and the question had me stumped for quite some time! Is anyone ever truly qualified?

While I completely recommend everyone to invest in the **Accredited Holistic Grooming Diploma** (please do, it's fab!), gaining the certificate is only one part of your life-long journey as a Holistic Groomer. Being qualified, certified and/or experienced in this way of grooming doesn't necessarily mean you are guaranteed to be operating holistically. That is based on what you do every time you get a new dog through your door. Never stop being the student. Remember that.

The important thing to know is that Holistic Grooming is a path that we all take at a different pace. As long as we continue to invest our time into developing our skills in observation, compassion and positive, force-free methods, we are all Holistic Groomers.

And of course, never underestimate the value of reading (the right books of course) – I have read SO many wonderful books and even though many of them cover the same topics, the beauty is that you get to learn things from another person's perspective.

Additionally, I recommend you volunteer your skills to local animal shelters as this is a fantastic way to develop and expand on all of the skills required in Holistic Grooming. What's more, you'll meet like-minded people and give something vitally important back to your community whilst you do it (shout out to my friend, Lorraine Jardine who founded Islay Dog Rescue - she works incredibly hard to help dogs who would otherwise be on death row).

Instead of asking *how* to be a Holistic Groomer, start by assessing whether you have the right ethics using the following checklist:

ACTIVITY

The Holistic Groomer Ethics:

- **I am a person who is passionate about preserving the health and wellbeing of animals and myself.**
- **I am a person with a genuine interest in how to help an animal feel more relaxed, content and happy when being groomed.**
- **I am a person who is eager to learn, and use only positive tools and techniques in my work with animals.**
- **I am a person who is dedicated to learning and embracing new ideas, so long as they are positive and beneficial to myself and to animals.**

- **I am a person who embraces change, and is willing to try new things.**

Ok I'm Ready, Where Do I Start?

Well as Julie Andrews once sang, "let's start at the very beginning – a very good place to start".

Some of the information in this book will make your tail wag, while others might have you clawing your hair out. It's true that Holistic Grooming can be complex, but the trick is to not overthink it too much. Trust me, it's worth the initial study-time.

So, you start with simply starting.

It's time to dig deeper into the very foundations of what makes a Holistic Groomer and how you, and your dogs can start reaping the benefits of it today.

2

THE HUMAN-CANINE BOND

"Dogs are not our whole life, but they make our lives whole."

— ROGER CARAS

Part One - Early Domestication

HOW WAS OUR INDUSTRY EVER POSSIBLE? IT'S AMAZING HOW far our relationship with dogs has come! But it wasn't until I began my transFURmation to Holistic Grooming that I realised just how relevant the very heritage and genetics of a dog is as we work towards creating a less stressful grooming environment.

I think it's important for us to travel back to the very beginning when *we think* early domestication took place, so that we can really appreciate just how much our more recent abilities in selective breeding has changed how we care for our furry friends.

When Dog Became Man's Best Friend

Dogs and humans are two peas in a fur covered pod.

As scavengers, it's speculated that wolves would have eaten the scraps left around campsites set up by early humans and benefited immensely from the warmth from the man-made fires thousands of years ago, but there is still a lot of debate amongst scientists.[1]

As the positive association with humans progressed (perhaps the earliest example of Classical Conditioning - otherwise known as Pavlov's Theory[2]), it would have been mutually beneficial for humans to make use of the wolves for their hunting abilities.

. . .

Here's what we *think* we know:

- **18,000-40,000 years ago** – Many scientists believe domestication of dogs began somewhere between this time-frame.
- **14,000 years ago** – dog fossils were found in Russia by archaeologists who came across a burial of a family, and their suspected pet dog.[3]
- **12,500 years ago** – dog fossils were found in East Asia dating back to 12,500 years ago.[4]
- **8,500 years ago** - Archaeologists discovered what is thought to be the earliest burial of a man and his dog. The significance of this finding is because history tells us that people from this period were often buried with sentimental objects, thus suggesting how important this dog must have been to his guardian.[5]
- **8000 years ago** - Cave paintings were discovered in the Arabian Desert, showing dogs on leashes and hunting for game with their human counterparts, proving that dogs were most definitely domesticated at this point in their evolution.[6]
- **1959** - Russian Scientist, Dmitri Konstantinocvich Belyaev, began his study of Silver Foxes, which would bring about a revelation in self-selection in domestication.[7]
- **1980** - The first ever "designer breed" emerged when Wally Conron of the Royal Guide Dog Association in Australia introduced the 'Labdradoodle', though this is later considered a big regret.[8]
- **Present Day** - the introduction of weird, and

mysterious doggy hybrids has emerged as the demand for "designer" breeds continue to rise bringing with them an array of health disorders.

What is Neoteny?

We're all suckers for a baby animal, right? Well, neoteny relates to our desire to keep those baby animals young and baby-like for as long as possible because it activates our maternal/paternal instinct to nurture, love, and protect.

A survey was given to guardians of French Bulldogs, Cairn Terriers, Chihuahuas and Cavalier King Charles Spaniels. Specifically, the guardians of the Bulldogs, Cavaliers and Chihuahuas said that they decided on choosing that breed because the dog was "cute", "baby-like" and "fashionable".[9]

It is our instinctive nature to look after babies that make neoteny in the breeding of domesticated dogs such a lucrative market. It's simply human nature, and we all play a big part to perpetuate it.

Did you know that the attributes that we consider 'cute' in an animal ignites the production of the loving hormones - oxytocin and serotonin - enhancing the bond that we share with them? How can this possibly be bad, right?

Selective breeding was first properly discovered when Russian Scientist, Dmitri Konstantinocvich Belyaev began his studies of wild Silver Foxes. Over just a short few decades he was able to fine-tune selective breeding to introduce a whole new, tamed species of Silver Fox. The selective breeding of this generation of foxes not only displayed juvenile characteristics, but retained cub-like physical features also. This was a revelation in the world of domestication, and one that continues to inspire scientists, and breeders to this day.[10]

It is thought that this initial discovery was to be the catalyst to our more challenging breed types, where the goal was to achieve more and more "cute" looking dogs - without much regard to the health of the animals involved, sadly. Even sadder still, we are continuing to see the introduction to strange and interesting breed mixes that appeal to this need for aesthetics over health.

What's more troubling in a more topical sense, was the announcement of BBC Three's new entrepreneurial documentary, '*Will My Puppies Make Me Rich?*' that was pitched by two young girls during the Covid-19 pandemic, when the price of buying a puppy sky-rocketed. The title alone is questionable as well as concerning, and one that many animal rights activists and welfare campaigners have been fighting to have shut down.

Part Two - Selective Breeding and Choosing The Right Breed

Bad Breeding Makes Grooming Difficult

Just as the BBC documentary mentioned above highlights, more and more people are looking for the next 'trending' dog breed, and it's causing some catastrophic consequences to the Pet Industry in general. As we continue to demand more cute-looking breeds, breeders are introducing new variations of breeds to the market to keep things fresh.

Whether it's the hypo-allergenic Aussie Doodle that is castrated before he's even 8 weeks old, or the 'forever puppy' concept of Chihuahuas long before them, the physical appearance of the domesticated dog seems to be more important to people than the physical health of their pet.

In addition to the range of health conditions that we are seeing in these mixes (think of the breathing difficulties in Brachycephalic dogs like Bulldogs and Pugs), groomers are also seeing a range of complex coat types that are almost impossible to groom without causing some form of discomfort or pain in the process - and are witnessing a variety of different behavioural issues added into the mix for good measure.

Holistic Grooming and commercial styling have never been more challenging.

HEALTHY PUPPIES START **With Responsible Breeders**

Some thoughts…

- Reputable breeders know the difference between a healthy dog breed and an unhealthy one, and would therefore not even so much as entertain the mixing of two unsuitable dogs and/or breeds purely for aesthetic purposes, and to make a quick buck.
- Reputable breeders are licensed and comply with the Animal Welfare Act 2006. They do not breed a bitch more than three times (appropriately spaced out) in her lifetime, and the quality of life the bitch has is not compromised in any way, either. She lives a happy, healthy life.
- Reputable breeders are not in the business to get rich quick, but instead are invested into preserving the Breed Standard of their chosen breed(s). They dedicate their time, money and resources into raising healthy, happy puppies, and do all the necessary checks to ensure that their health is never compromised in the future.
- Reputable breeders will be extremely cautious when choosing a family to home one of their puppies – families should be vetted, and screened to ensure their lifestyle is suitable for their breed.
- Reputable breeders will welcome any, and all questions from a prospective dog guardian, and provide a contract that includes an agreement to take

back a puppy in the instance the families circumstance regrettably change.

Sadly, however, there are still many backstreet breeders, puppy farms, and accidental pregnancies all over the world, making it virtually impossible to preserve the health and wellbeing of all the dogs involved from birth. I use the word 'accidental' loosely.

The significance of the puppy development stages to grooming

In addition to breeding and raising puppies, knowledgeable breeders should understand the importance of the socialisation of dogs during the very early puppy development stages. Educating breeders on canine behaviour, communication, and puppy development prior to them planning their first litter is a crucial part of the process, and one I thoroughly enjoy investing time into.

Areas I cover in my 'Puppy Prepare' Packages include:

1. **Genetics/Heritage** – healthy dogs create healthy puppies. Think lineage, think genetics, think hereditary traits. It's not just about mum and dad. It takes a whole family to raise good puppies, and it starts before those puppies even appear in the womb!

2. **Prenatal Care** – how the mother is cared for during her pregnancy is significant. Allowing her to feel relaxed and safe throughout her term whilst also

tending to her needs physically, emotionally and mentally are all crucial to the pups she bears. Puppies are already feeding off the mother's hormones, therefore a stressed mother results in stressed puppies.

3. **Observing the early days** – puppies require guidance from their mother to build confidence, but they also learn 'how to be a dog' through playing with their littermates, too. Things like bite inhibition and testing the boundaries are not uncommon, and should not be interfered with by a concerned breeder. The mother of the pups will often correct bad behaviour, which can often be misinterpreted by a breeder as a mother rejecting the pup in some way. Caution not to intervene with this natural process is recommended, but be mindful to recognise if it's going too far, too.

4. **Socialisation Plans** - the breeder has a responsibility to begin introducing each puppy to life as a pet and all that this involves. That means introducing them to objects, sounds, textures, smells, tastes, people, handling, light grooming, health checking… all of these aspects are things a puppy must be carefully exposed to before they leave the nest. Grooming always starts with the mother of the pup.

5. **Microchipping and Vet Care** – preparing a puppy for his first experiences with pet professionals is crucial when it comes to first impressions. As a microchip implanter, I visit the Breeder's home and perform the procedure in the puppies own comforts at around 5-weeks. I take every precaution to ensure the puppies

first experience of getting jagged is positive using positive reinforcement, praise, and gentle handling. The next appointment will be at the Veterinary Practice, yet careful consideration of what practice the breeder goes to means making sure the environment is as stress-free as possible.

Keep it positive.

Myth Buster: puppies shouldn't be groomed until they are 6 months old (SIGH!)

Grooming starts from the moment the puppy is born, and should continue throughout the puppy development stages and on through the remainder of the dog's life. *Professional grooming* can – and should - be introduced as soon as the puppy is able to venture outside.

In addition to this, I advise that guardians should try to visit their chosen groomer (just to say hello) once, or twice on the lead up to their puppy's first visit, to gradually familiarise the environment to them in a non-invasive way.

Remember, positive socialisation that starts early will increase the chances of a puppy growing up to be resilient, happy and content in later life (albeit, it's not solely dependent on this fact – more on this later).

Professional *Styling* can be introduced when the puppy has been successfully introduced, and desensitised to the objects, sounds, and demands of a more intricate appointment but may have to be performed over a few shorter sessions initially.

WHY BREED CHOICE MATTERS – a note to Guardians

The choice of breed should come down to foresight and risk-assessment if nothing else. Essentially, given that it's your responsibility to fully care for your dog, have you thought about how much money you will need to spend on Grooming and Vet bills each year? And how demanding the coat will be to maintain in between?

Are you ready for the commitment?

Note: I encourage all dog guardians to attend a masterclass with their groomer to be shown how to successfully maintain a healthy skin and coat (especially for the more demanding coat-types).

Whilst it's incredibly difficult to resist a pair of puppy dog eyes, the demand for strange and mysterious dog breeds will continue to snowball out of control if we don't make a conscious effort to stop the demand for it in its tracks, because when dogs get ill, and people can't afford – or don't want – to care for them, we know what happens.

The rise of dogs in shelters has rocketed over the years, proving that the expectation of what having a puppy involves often doesn't match the reality, especially when the onset of numerous physical, behavioural and neurological conditions emerges. I fear the pandemic of 2020/21 won't have helped in this, as people scramble to get pups for companionship and distraction before realising that they cannot afford and/or don't have the time to care for them properly when work resumes as normal.[11]

Think smart.

Due diligence, research, and understanding are the very first steps in buying a puppy – and without first ticking off those three things, a guardian is failing to prepare.

3

THE HISTORY OF GROOMING

"If you always do what you've always done, you'll always get what you've always got."

— HENRY FORD

BEFORE WE GET INTO THE MECHANICS OF HOLISTIC GROOMING itself, I think it's important that we understand the history of the very industry we have decided to make our life's work... so let's start with what grooming is and where it came from.

"Grooming is an ancient practice that we all do instinctively."

— STEPHANIE ZIKMANN

I watched an interview featured on the Groomers Connexions YouTube channel[1], where two well-respected groomers spoke about the grooming trade and how it has evolved throughout the years.

During the conversation, a statement was made that caught my attention:

"When we compare our industry to other pet industries, ours is very young."

Our industry may be young, but the practice of grooming itself is actually very old.

When we begin to learn the heritage of grooming itself, it's evident that our industry's definition of what it means has been diluted quite considerably. In addition to this, the practice of grooming has evolved to cater to the ever-growing aesthetic needs of our more complexed coats. As a result, we now have what we might refer to as 'Professional Styling'.

A lucrative business, with a slightly different purpose to its predecessor.

Therefore, I think it's important we understand that there are actually TWO histories of Commercial Grooming, both of which are quite significant in our understanding of what the more recent, 'Holistic Grooming', might involve.

To summarise, we have:

1. **Grooming and Allo-Grooming** – the natural, instinctive behaviour that all animals share.
2. **Professional Styling** – a profession that combines

styling techniques, with basic grooming requirements to achieve Breed Standard, Show and Creative Styles.

If you are like me then history is probably not something that interests you much, but bring animals into the equation, and suddenly my ears prick with excitement!

Indulge me…

Part One – Grooming and Allo Grooming

Our animals have been showing us what grooming is since the beginning of time, proving that not only is it a very ancient and instinctual practice, but also one that helps to develop family relationships and preserve overall wellness, too.

'Allo-grooming' by definition is, *"the grooming of one animal by another of the same species"* – a term devised by Zoologists back in the 1960s. Furthermore, it translates to *"grooming another."*[2]

The act of allo-grooming involves plucking, picking, biting, stroking and licking gestures - otherwise known as grooming gestures - performed for very specific purposes.

Fun Fact – Monkeys in Japan love a spa day!

BBC Earth once published a documentary featuring 'monkey spas' in Japan. It told the story of how native monkeys came to learn the benefits of having a hot bath through observing local

Japanese people who would often spend time bathing in natural hot-bath spots within the forests.[3]

The monkeys are seen to be relaxing in the water, proving that the concept of spa days is one that not only humans can appreciate!

This revelation could be all the proof we need to consider that our approach towards grooming in a commercial setting to date, is missing an element of relaxation that could change the way our animals feel about their visit to the grooming salon.

It's definitely something the Holistic Groomer should take into consideration when planning how to operate their business and adapt their approach, even if you don't go on to serve iced lemon water as part of the session!

What's the purpose of grooming in the wild?

There are a few benefits:

- Physical Health Preservation
- Emotional Health Preservation
- Relationship Building

Let's take a closer look.

1. Physical Health Preservation:

Did you know that self-medication could be considered an extension of grooming in the wild?

Many animals have been known to treat skin conditions, sores, and injuries through the application/rubbing of meditative plants onto the affected areas as part of their self-grooming routines and allo-grooming rituals.

Additionally, some zoologists refer to 'comfort behaviours' as a series of grooming, stretching, dust bathing and sham dust-bathing activities.

Comfort behaviours are carried out by all animals from an early age, with the purpose of hygiene, cleaning wounds, reducing heart rate, and thermoregulation.[4]

This is interesting if we want to understand more in-depth how grooming in general can be more of a positive experience to animals, rather than a negative one that many dogs -and their handlers - often dread.

2. Emotional Health Preservation:

Science now reveals that most animals can feel many (if not all) the primary emotions that humans can, therefore it goes without saying that Holistic Grooming benefits an animal emotionally, just as it does for humans.

> *"One-way animals reduce their anxiety levels is through grooming, hugging, and stroking themselves. Both wild and domesticated animals defer feeding in favour of self-grooming when they are subjected to physical or emotional stress."*[5]

> — CINDY ENGEL, WILD HEALTH

3. Relationship Building:

Grooming is also used in the wild to strengthen social structures within the family unit. Scientists and Zoologists have observed many different species across the Animal Kingdom who use grooming techniques to express affection, and show respect to their family hierarchy.

To further highlight just how effective, and important grooming is in the preservation of health and wellbeing, let's briefly look at some of these animals:

Wolves

Wolves groom members of their family pack to strengthen family bonds and to remove dirt and debris from the coat.

> *"Wolves are visibly affectionate to one another, and can often be seen engaging in mutual grooming sessions, or lying close to each other and maybe even touching - especially the breeding pair."*[6]

— TONI SHELBOURNE, THE TRUTH ABOUT WOLVES AND DOGS

Primates

If the Monkey Spa documentary wasn't proof enough that primates love being groomed, Jane Goodall also spent years observing Chimpanzee's during her time in Gombe Forest.

"Friendships are maintained and poor relationships are improved by the most important of all friendly behaviours – social grooming...this enables adult chimpanzees to spend long hours in friendly, relaxed physical contact. A session may last more than an hour as the participants work their way, with soothing movements of their fingers, over every inch of each other's bodies. Grooming is used to calm tense or nervous companions, and mothers can often quieten restless or distressed infants in the same way."[7]

— JANE GOODALL, REASON FOR HOPE

Wood Mice

Female wood mice take their personal hygiene very seriously and demand that the males groom themselves prior to mating. Mating will not ensue until the female is satisfied that the male is adequately (squeaky) clean.[8]

Ha – you've gotta love wood mice!

Rats

Darlene Francis and Michael Meaney conducted research into rats, and through their observations noticed that those who were licked and groomed frequently by their mothers were calmer and more resilient to stress as they matured. They also had stronger immune systems.[9]

Inter-species grooming

In Brazil, allo-grooming occurs between black caracaras and bare-skinned tapirs, and between pale-winged trumpeters and grey brocket deer, with the purpose of removing parasites[10]. Lovely.

Of course, allo-grooming doesn't necessarily mean that grooming has to be between same-species for it to be beneficial.

Therefore, it's not far-fetched to think that it's possible for grooming between humans and dogs (or cats) to be a relaxing and enjoyable experience when carried out with a more holistic approach in mind.

Domesticated Dogs

Myth Buster: Cats self-groom, dogs don't.

Wrong!

The domesticated dog will lick, nibble and often roll in grass as a means to self-groom, and it's believed that this is their way of removing parasites and/or other foreign bodies from their fur, to soothe a pain and/or itch and to comfort themselves and/or others.

I have also wondered whether a dog is more inclined to roll in grass to remove the synthetic chemicals of our fragranced products, particularly post-groom.

Dogs have also been known to clean other animal members of his family unit through licking and nibbling (more commonly around the eyes and ears), and extending the gesture to his human companions too (so it may not just be the salt from your skin after all)!

A Note On Licking

Zoologists observing animals throughout the years have discovered that not only can licking help to self-soothe an animal, but that it can also aid in cleaning and healing of wounds to free them from infection.[11]

> *"The wounds of adult male baboons are carefully groomed by females, and this, along with self-grooming and licking, helps the healing process. Many species, such as primates, canids, felids and rodents, lick wounds. In most species studied, wound-licking is an innate response to injury, not one learned through observation."*
>
> — CINDY ENGEL, WILD HEALTH

In fact, a dog's saliva is capable of killing all sorts of nasty bacteria, including Staphylococcus, Escherichia coli and Streptococcus.[12] Yummy!

The discovery of the healing qualities of dog saliva dates back to Ancient Egyptian times, when it was used as an effective alternative to today's antibacterial cream.[13]

Furthermore, after analysing saliva from Labradors and Beagles, researchers at the University of Birmingham discovered that dog saliva contains antimicrobial enzymes, proteins (lysozymes and immunoglobulins) and antimicrobial peptides. Additionally, they found that the saliva contained other proteins similar to histatins (a compound found in human saliva that speeds up wound healing by promoting the migration of new skin cells).[14]

That being said, it is still worth being mindful that excessive licking has been known to actually *aggravate* infection, thus spreading it quicker. Therefore, it should not be relied upon as a cure for health disorders, but rather used as a sign that we can observe early, to prompt us in seeking Veterinary assistance before the underlying cause advances.

Humans Groom Too

Bathing, washing hair, playing with our hair, scratching, tickling, massaging, plucking, and squeezing are all forms of grooming - and so is massage therapy!

During my research for this book, I came across an interesting fellow who was inspired by the way wild animals groom themselves. He believed that true grooming (the technique of pressing, nipping and stretching the skin with our fingers, and hands) could straighten out wrinkles, and make us look younger for longer. When I went back to get the source, it was gone (not gonna lie, it could well have been a dream!).

But let's take massage as an example:

Massage is great for our circulation because it eases tension, keeps our muscles supple, and helps blood flow but there are additional benefits in the physical sense of touch during a massage that we often take for granted.

Evidence now suggests that our advancement in technology is replacing social and physical contact with catastrophic effect. A society deprived of physical contact would result in an increase of violence, less trust between individuals, less economic gain, an increase in disease, and a weakening of immune systems. There would be non-existent team dynamics, a decrease in emotional intimacy, less compassionate people, a less intelligent society, and a massive increase in mental health disorders along the way.[15] This really is devastating, and a real eye-opener when it comes to the statistics of mental health disorders across the globe. So, if we want to look after ourselves, and our animals, Holistic Grooming is most definitely the way forward!

Grooming Is NOT Styling

Grooming (in its truest sense) is in fact any form of physical contact that we (an animal) make to enhance our health, and wellbeing.

I believe that Holistic Grooming isn't just the act of keeping oneself clean, but also includes the many other alternative therapies that exist today. Therefore, grooming *is* comfort behaviour all animals of the Animal Kingdom instinctively do to also strengthen our relationships and express love for one another.

Grooming is beautiful, don't you think?

Grooming Is Therapy

Below is a list of some techniques we can use in the salon (or at home) that I consider to be an extension of, and great enhancer to Holistic Grooming:

- TTouch
- Bowens Technique
- Myofascial Release
- Trigger Point Therapy
- Canine Massage

Can you imagine the difference we could make if we all learned how to embrace the healing aspect of grooming in our professional salons, and at home too?

I can because I practice it every day, and watch the magic unfold.

Part Two – Commercial Grooming

"There is beauty in simplicity."

— UNKNOWN

Records of grooming between human and canine officially date back to the middle ages, where dogs were predominantly owned to serve a specific working purpose to their masters and were typically a symbol of social status.

Additionally, dogs were very useful in tending to other needs too including vermin control, protection of livestock and, of course, companionship, all of which required the dog to stay clean and healthy.

. . .

EARLY GROOMING

Kennel boys would live with and care for the dogs, ensuring they were brushed and cleaned to enable them to efficiently carry out their working duties with ease.

Fast forward to the 16th Century, and we can find evidence in portraits and paintings to suggest that the pet grooming industry began to grow in demand, and highlight a more aesthetic requirement.

The pet dog (as opposed to the working dog) concept was soon to be introduced by wealthy ladies of the manor, who would pose with lapdogs (who were typically always well-groomed).

Despite this, larger dogs such as Poodles (also referred to as 'water retrievers') were still required to carry on their hunting duties; specifically, catching ducks. Paintings showed more intricate styles of their fur, requiring extensive scissoring and clipping. For example, the style that we know as 'continental' was specifically designed to protect the Poodle's vital organs with thick, curly hair, whilst shaving the rest to make swimming and coat maintenance much more manageable[16].

19th Century

Then in the 19th Century royalty truly kickstarted a fashion trend that would result in the thriving industry that Professional Styling is today!

The Kennel Club, UK as formed in 1873 - followed closely over the years by other organisations including the SCC (France), ENCI (Italy), American Kennel Club, and Canadian

Kennel Club – very much decide what makes a dog a good representation of that particular type (Breed Standard specifications); considering their skeletal and musculature structure, gait and movement, coat, personality and mannerisms all in the mix.

At this time, dogs became more accessible to everyone, and the demand to have them styled to show off their Breed Standard meant that styling became a truly lucrative business.

In the 1960s, Creative Grooming was first seen through the trend in dying a dog's coat in psychedelic colours, with some even showcasing plastic flowers that had been stuck on the coat with glue![17]

Present Day

Since then, the grooming industry has built up a reputation as being one of skill, fashion and art. It attracts media attention all across the globe, and has seen he rise of styling competitions where top show-groomers battle it out to become 'Next Top Stylist' as they showcase some of the most creative, and imaginative styles.

Big business, indeed!

4

THE GROOMING INDUSTRY

"Almost every successful person begins with two beliefs: the future can be better than the present, and I have the power to make it so."

— DAVID BROOKS

THE TRUTH IS OUR GROOMING CURRICULUM IS MOSTLY outdated and old-fashioned, and it's our duty to ensure that the information we are teaching students is up-to-date and relevant, based on what the facts tell us.

When I have referred to this topic in the past I have been attacked, and ridiculed by some people who believe that on the contrary the grooming industry itself has come a long way. And it has – the advancement of styling equipment and tools alone is enough to warrant that credit. The better designs of our more modern tools are worth mentioning because that really does make all the difference in the productivity of our roles as stylists.

Part One – Professional Styling

The 'Dog' In Dog Grooming

But what about the 'dog' in the dog grooming? Have we advanced our own knowledge in how we understand and communicate with dogs? Do we know the difference between a "firm" approach, and a "dominant" approach?

As I've said, Commercial Grooming is doing a great job at establishing itself as a lucrative industry in the ever-growing market that is Pets. That much is true. And from a solely super-ficial perspective, we seem to be ticking all the boxes.

But Holistic Grooming is all about digging deeper, remember?

> *"Our relationship with other animals is a complex, ambiguous, challenging, and frustrating affair, and we must continually reassess how we should interact with our nonhuman kin. Part of this reassessment involves asking difficult questions, and making sure our actions match our understandings and beliefs."*
>
> — MARC BEKOFF, THE EMOTIONAL LIVES OF ANIMALS

Therefore, what we knew 30, 20, even 10 years ago (specifi-cally when it comes to emotions and behaviour, and the poten-tial impact grooming has to the psychological, and emotional part of the dog), is certainly just a drop in the ocean of what we now know today, and will continue to discover as the years go on.

What Training Taught Me

Practical Training is fast-paced, stressful and often over-crowded due to demand. That was certainly my experience when I invested in a 30-day intensive course within a busy salon, and I know I'm not the only one.

Additionally, my training had a real focus on the END result – what Breed or Pet Standard trim was I intending to complete in 1.5 hours? What did I need to do to get the job done in as little time possible? What handling restraints would I need to use to keep the dog from jumping off the table? And so on.

The process to get from A-Z also had some significant terminology, that I believe makes the purpose of Commercial Grooming crystal clear:

1. We learn how to *prep* a dog to allow a good finish.
2. We learn what *handling restraints* we need to *keep the dog in place.*
3. We learn what tools we need to use to achieve the perfect *finish.*
4. We learn how to do it efficiently to keep our time down.

Everything the trainee student is taught is for the purpose of achieving as close to perfect as possible – the very words ("prep", and "finish") that are used, highlight the real emphasis on just that. But that's just business at the end of the day, and whether we like it or not the commercial grooming industry has been transformed over the years into an art form that requires dedication, talent and real guts to master.

Breeders, our very own Kennel Clubs, and Show Exhibitions such as Crufts, are all adding to the pressure Commercial Groomers have in their roles, because dog guardians naturally expect their dogs to look a certain way, and I don't believe they realise how difficult that can be for the average pet dog.

ACTIVITY

Without any input from you, I want you to ask 10 different people the following question:

> *"What do you think a dog groomer does, and what does it involve exactly?"*

Using the list below, write the number of people who each respond with this, or a similar answer.

Dog grooming is/ involves:

- **Styling a dog**
- **Bathing a dog to get them clean and make them smell good**
- **Taking care of the dog's health and wellbeing**
- **Training a dog to enjoy being groomed, being able to handle a dog safely, knowing how to identify early signs of illness or injury, making sure a dog is**

free from parasites, ensuring a dog is clean, happy and healthy, styling a dog to make him look good.

Now read over the numbers you've collected.

Are you surprised with your results?

When I did this exercise, can you guess how many said anything close to number four?

ONE! And that was my husband, who probably watches me work so hard with our own dogs at home (we have FOUR!).

I found my results scary, and concerning because it proved to me that our industry is simply not doing enough to show the world our value. Opportunities to educate the public are scarce, and anytime we do get publicity, it's for entertainment purposes only, in fact there's a BBC Grooming Competition airing right now, as I type!

Alas, we must remember that the majority of TV Programmes are for entertainment purposes, and not a realistic reflection of what an industry entails.

Basic Behaviour Is Covered

I think it's important to say that while Commercial Grooming focuses on Professional Styling, it does cover the very basics of behaviour. *When* it's covered, and *what* is covered is where it gets tricky…

First of all, behaviour is usually an add-on basic course that comes with your initial training investment (in fact, it was one of the most appealing selling points to the training venue I attended). But what I soon discovered was that behaviour was a term used loosely, and what we were taught was limited (very limited), and completely outdated.

The first thing that I was taught by my (anonymous) tutor in regards to behaviour was,

"We are groomers, not behaviourists and we are paid to get the job done."

The second thing was that,

"Aggressive dogs aren't worth your career. Refer them to an experienced groomer."

The third was,

"All dogs need to be secured on the table for safety, and when something isn't working, add something else."

I suspect that this may just be the general way things are taught for efficiency in a busy commercial grooming setting, but it was still heart-breaking to me because I expected *more*.

It's important to also note that it's also possible to come across some truly amazing tutors who (at their discretion) cover behaviour far more in-depth – treasure them!

Typically, however, Commercial Grooming is about efficiency through the control of the animals in our care, and a basic understanding of behaviour is required for theory purposes - nothing more, nothing less.

An Aesthetic Approach

Generally speaking, the role of styling is to achieve a Creative, Breed or Pet Standard trim whether it is for Commercial, Competition and/or Show purposes.

Professional styling requires an immense amount of knowledge about the dog from an aesthetic perspective:

- What are the dog's breed standard specifications?
- What was the dog bred for?
- How is he formed physiologically?
- How does he move?
- How does his fur grow?
- Are there any 'faults' that need attention?
- How symmetrical are the legs?
- How is the angulation, and does it flatter the dog's shape?
- Does the style suit the dog's personality?
- Is the face showing expression?

And so on.

Styling is a very technical approach, and one that requires an immense amount of studying of the anatomy of the dog to understand the mechanics of the gait, the posture and the overall way he is formed.

The aim of the stylist is to achieve a flawless finish. This requires careful preparation, a sharp eye, the right tools and the right techniques to achieve. The minimum a commercial groomer *must* be able to achieve is "acceptable commercial standard" though - what that means though, I haven't a Scooby Dooby Doo!

Can Anyone Style An Animal?

The simple answer to that question? No, not without official training, study and lots of practice (I'm not gonna lie – styling is bloody tricky)! But anyone with patience, and a genuine interest in the art of styling can most definitely learn how to style a dog.

But remember to shop around, and:

- Attend a reputable school that is accredited through an awarding body like iPET.
- Ask for plenty of demonstrations and one-to-one tuition from a good stylist.
- Attend as many seminars as possible.
- Find stylists that inspire you – and whose values you respect (I drove a 13-hour round trip just to attend a seminar with 'Asian Fusion' Queen, Riza Wisnom – and I even managed to snap a selfie).

Truth be told, I'm not a great stylist. That doesn't mean I'm not committed to learning how to style a dog, but it does mean I'm not as committed to styling a dog for aesthetic purposes as I am about grooming a dog for welfare purposes. We all have a choice at the end of the day, and it's about choosing a market that reflects your goals.

A Quick Note On Styling For Guardians and Grooming Enthusiasts

Lockdown 2020 resulted in many guardians taking to clippers like stones to water. Groomers were faced with some challenging fixer-uppers when the closure of many businesses forced desperate guardians to try it themselves. And it wasn't all fun, and games either – many dogs were injured in the attempt, highlighting it was actually no laughing matter.

Styling should most definitely be left to qualified and/or experienced professionals, and not attempted by an untrained guardian, or someone who has decided an online course for £20 on Groupon is substantial enough to start scissoring. Step away from the Facebook ad!

Just remember, grooming and styling are completely different.

If you are serious about learning how to style however, I do recommend you follow the advice from this chapter.

An Outdated Approach

How many times have you heard the following phrases?

"She just bit from nowhere – I swear this dog is evil!"

or

"He's a Chow Chow - they're a really aggressive breed."

or

"He growls, so you need to muzzle him to stop him from biting you."

And it's ok if you have said these things yourself, because I certainly did when I first started grooming professionally – it's what, and how I was taught. I didn't know what I know today, and that's why we should always be learning, as I've already mentioned.

The truth is, though, that these statements are not helpful because they come from a place of misunderstanding and miscommunication. As we delve more into canine psychology, it will become clear why stereotyping and labels often stop us from reading between the lines.

We can often set ourselves up for failure from the moment a dog enters the salon through labelling and stereotyping alone. We make assumptions and we behave and react according to what we think will happen, rather than what is actually the case.

But it's not just the curriculum that encourages this sort of approach.Many of the legislations that exist still support outdated beliefs about certain breeds and behaviours, which we will discuss in more detail in a later chapter.

It's hard to stop labelling dogs because it's undeniably a part of human culture, and whilst Holistic Grooming aims to help the student come away from stereotyping, it's important not to be too hard on ourselves in the process.

Compassion to ourselves, and others, goes a long way.

True Story

When I was growing up, I battled with a mental health condition. I was alone in doing this, because at that time mental health was still very much a taboo subject.

My mum worked in a Doctor's Surgery and thought it was best that I deal with my feelings at home, in fear that people might judge me wrongly, or that it would hinder my employment opportunities (at that time, she was probably right).

It took me 7 years of struggling before I finally asked for professional help.

Even then it was still very much a taboo subject, but it's amazing the difference now – 18 years later - has made!

I guess the point I'm trying to make is it takes time to change the status quo, and there's bound to be some ripples along the way.

Handling Restraints Keep Us And The Dog Safe

When it comes to working sharp and dangerous tools around moving, living animals surely the use of handling restraints is a good idea? This thought process is probably why our curriculum encourages us to use them so much, and sure it makes total sense for a person to if they only understand the very basics of canine behaviour.

Some of us might think that using handling restraints helps us to avoid risks, but really, risks are everywhere, and it's more about choosing which risks you are happy working with. I'm not gonna lie - it's simply not possible to create a completely risk-free grooming environment (even through Holistic Grooming), just as it's not possible to carry out a completely stress-free groom!

But what I will say is, that some things we are trained to do, *sometimes* *add* more risks, because we get lazy and fail to pick up on signs of doggy distress early enough. Let me explain…

The most popular way a commercial groomer might lessen risk/increase safety is using one or more handling restraints/aids.

EXAMPLE:

A groomer might prevent an "aggressive" dog from biting her hand by controlling his neck, head, and body using a 'Groomers Helper'.

This device stops all directions of movement in the dog, and helps the groomer to complete a groom "safely".

But not always.

When we aren't mindful about how we introduce these tools, when and how we use them, it can be counter-productive, and cause the animal unnecessary harm. This is why my list of handling tools is very limited, and doesn't include The Groomers Helper.

When we use such tools without careful consideration, they can actually *induce* erratic behaviours in the animal, leading to either outbursts of frustration, anger, and rage, or the emotional and physical shut down of the animal completely. This is more common than you might think.

When Dogs Attack Out Of Nowhere

If we restrain a fearful dog on the grooming table for two hours without careful introduction, there is no doubt it will cause an escalation of behaviours.

It can take some dogs days (even weeks!) to return to a parasympathetic state, and what's more, each visit thereafter will continue to escalate behaviours much quicker, which can result in a more unpredictable aggressive outburst.

EXAMPLE

When a dog is feeling particularly anxious of a High Velocity Dryer, a groomer may use a belly AND neck strap to keep the dog from jumping off the table and hurting himself (or the groomer).

However, the use of these two devices together causes energy disruption, and also eliminates one of the survival responses (flee), thus causing two consequences:

1. **The inability to release stress in a way that avoids conflict (stretching, shaking-off, or removing himself from the "threat").**
2. **An escalation of behaviours due to an emotional overload (also known as exceeding threshold), most likely resulting in a FIGHT response (lunging, snarling, clawing, and biting).**

Therefore, ask yourself:

How do I prevent suppressed emotions in the grooming environment?

We introduce CHOICE – more on this later.

Holistic Grooming is About An Alternative Outlook

It's about educating ourselves more on *why* a dog is behaving this way first, before looking at how we might manage the situation.

Think:

Why am I using a neck strap?

Why am I using a Groomers Helper?

Why do I need to hold the dog in place?

Why is the dog not happy on the grooming table right now?

When a groomer fails to ask WHY, she increases her risk of being bitten or scratched, maybe not today, but next time. So start asking yourself those questions – please! Then, do something (positive) about it.

True Story

I recently found myself engrossed in quite a heated debate on social media with another groomer over my approach to grooming, and I was told that I was "reckless" in my handling because I often don't use restraints.

My defence was that I had never been bitten at work, despite predominantly grooming dogs that have been deemed "aggressive" in the past. I stood by the fact that this is because my approach works.

However, a couple of days later, something shocking happened: I was bitten.

BY MY OWN DOG (on my backside of all the places!).

Yet, it was through my own negligence that I forgot to separate my two Tibetan Mastiffs at dinner time, which in turn resulted in a food war that I happened to get in the way of.

I couldn't believe it, though. *ME:* Mrs 'I'm-a-holistic-groomer-and-have-never-been-bitten' had been bitten, and what's worse, by a dog that I share my home and my life with, whom I know and understand. The truth is though, it was *my* fault!

Mortified puts it mildly, but it was a lesson well learned! Don't get cocky. Nothing, and nobody is invincible.

It's extremely easy to make a mistake, to miscalculate, or to momentarily forget about something. So, whilst I truly believe that Holistic Grooming should involve less (sometimes even ZERO) handling restraints (for reasons I'll explain more in-depth later), it still has risks when we fail to **pay attention**.

HANDLING **Restraints Make Money**

Let's not forget that Handling Restraint manufacturers make a lot (A LOT) of money in the Pet Industry too – it's a HUGE market, and one that will be around for as long as domesticated dogs are (as in forever!).

And there are SO many to choose from, some better than others. All of them however, if used incorrectly (or inappropriately) can in fact *increase* our risk of injury and harm for both handler, and animal if we're not careful (and I'm not just talking physically either).

The only problem I have with handling restraints in the commercial grooming environment (and at home with guardians too) is that there is simply not enough instruction and/or demonstrations being done on how and when to use them safely.

And while I genuinely do believe that *some* can help to make our jobs easier; I think we should be careful not to use them as an alternative to safe observation, communication, and handling – topics we will go into more detail in other chapters.

That's good and well Stephanie but I'm a groomer, not a trainer or a dog whisperer, and I'm not paid to spend time reading a dog (remember the statement from my old tutor?).

Well, actually…

The Benefits Of Being More Than Just A "Groomer"

Whilst we might not get paid enough for what we do (that's a conversation for later), whether we care to admit it or not, we *are* trainers, behaviourists and 'dog psychologists' as well as groomers. Or at least we should be *striving* to be.

During an interview about Holistic Grooming on L.A Podcaster, Susan Hope Light's show, 'Doggy Dojo' for dog guardians, I spoke about the danger that groomers (guardians, and other professionals) expose themselves to when they don't understand how dogs communicate and express their emotions. You can listen to the episode via the link in Resources.

We often forget that hazards are everywhere. Or, we believe that a couple of handling restraints are going to prevent anything bad from happening, when that's not always the case!

Hell, as I've said already, we are working sharp objects, handling every sensitive part of the animal in front of us, operating potentially life-threatening equipment (drying cabinets, anyone?), ALL WHILST THE ANIMAL IS VERY MUCH CONSCIOUS! If you want to put things even more into perspective, Vets at least work with sharp tools while the dog is under sedation therefore, they can't move unexpectedly!

So learning to know all that we can about how a dog thinks, acts, and communicates can only help us be more prepared right? (The answer is yes!).

Commercial Grooming Could Be More Valuable

All commercial groomers feel overworked, misunderstood, and underpaid – it's true that our jobs are often strenuous, emotional, traumatic, and unpleasant. But that doesn't mean that we should all be entitled to a wage rise right away.

For things to change we must be prepared to *make* changes! We can do that in two ways:

1. Raise the bar in industry standards.
2. Then, start telling the world what we **actually** do.

Again, ask yourself:

Are we really succeeding in showing the world our value?

Lastly, Creative Grooming Has *A* Place

We tapped into Creative Grooming when looking at our history, so this is not an industry that is new to us by any means. This topic attracts a lot of media attention, and many are intrigued by the skills required in some of the more intricate and advanced creations. But before we get into the pros and cons let me tell you a story…

True Story

Back in 2018, I signed up for my first (and coincidently, last) creative grooming course at an award-winning salon about an hour away from where I lived.

I was excited.

Glitter, hair-dye, sticky gems and nail polish were amongst the different tools we used that day on the dogs that were volunteered by their guardians.

Whilst I had fun, I did notice a few things even before I'd ventured out on the path towards training in canine behaviour:

- *The dogs were visibly uncomfortable with the process of having their fur dyed and nails painted. In fact, they clearly hated it.*
- *The products were deemed 'dog safe', but not 100% dog safe as per the labels.*
- *The whole thing was a time-consuming process... even I was getting restless!*

While I agree with some groomers, that creative grooming is a great way to explore our imagination and express our feelings, I also must agree that it poses a real risk in encouraging people to objectify their animals, and take anthropomorphism to a more concerning level (don't shoot me down just yet!). Hear me out...

You might just be the most attentive and loving stylist who would never dream of doing anything to hurt your animal (I believe you by the way), but it may be worth considering alternative ways of being creative that don't involve as many risks. For example, I know of many Synthetic Dog Competitions for Creative Grooming which I believe, is the perfect compromise.

Whilst we can debate about it 'til we (or the dogs) are blue in the face; it's about asking ourselves the following questions:

Is creative grooming on living animals really necessary?

What is the purpose of creative grooming?

How does it benefit the animals?

Can the animal live without it?

What message is it giving to children?

In an interview for The BBC, a spokesperson for the RSPCA said, *"The extreme pampering of pets sends out a very worrying message that they [dogs] could be viewed as novelty accessories rather than as intelligent, sentient animals."*[1]

Regardless of our own views, if we want to open or operate within a practice that is truly holistic, we need to remember that grooming should ultimately be about the preservation of health and wellbeing. Therefore, considering the time involved in some of the more advanced creative grooming styles (sometimes up to SIX hours!), the additional risks of using bleach and other hair dying products, the implication of excessive bathing and/or clip offs over an extended period of time, and the possible effect it can have to the overall wellbeing of an animal not carefully desensitised to the process or the attention that comes with it, *extreme* creative grooming is not advisable from a Holistic Grooming perspective (which is what this book is about after-all).

PS. I don't believe a splash of coloured chalk on the ears and/or tail is going to do your dog significant psychological harm. Holistic Grooming is about compromise for the greater good.

Part Two – Choosing A Groomer Or Tutor

"Experience is overrated. Some people say they have twenty years, when in reality, they only have one year's experience, repeated twenty times."

— STEPHEN COVEY

I believe Holistic Grooming is an approach that will only enhance our industry, and make us more credible. It is an advanced education into the areas of grooming that our industry is yet to catch up on. We can easily apply what we learn in Holistic Grooming into what we learn about styling; making our business more relaxing and thus, more efficient than we could have ever imagined.

With that in mind it's important to realise that while we can seek to learn the holistic side through books like this one, and courses like The Holistic Grooming Diploma (see Resources), it is still extremely important to find a reputable training provider to teach us the fundamentals of operating a Commercial Grooming Business; specifically when it comes to our practical styling capabilities.

So, let's talk about choosing the right person to show you the ropes.

Are All Stylists, and Tutors Good?

As you'll know the grooming industry is still an unregulated industry (2021), which means that any Tom, Dick or Harriet can learn to professionally style a dog and ply their trade to earn money from it.

There are obvious pros and cons to this:

PROS:

1. People like me, who have undergone training but have not gone on to obtain an official grooming qualification can still operate professionally (thank Dog!).
2. Holistic Groomers can use this time to raise awareness, update and expand on the current curriculum content to include other topics and make the entire approach more holistic *before* making it regulated.

CONS:

1. Anyone can open up as a professional groomer and/or training salon and teach (and charge a fortune) others how to become a Professional Stylist (eek!).
2. Many training facilities aren't routinely (if at all) spot-checked, therefore students couldvery well be wasting thousands of pounds on training in wholly inappropriate facilities (I did).
3. It puts our animals in an even more vulnerable position due to inexperienced and/or unqualified groomers and/or guardians who don't know what they're doing - but do it anyway (alas, such is the story of lockdown as mentioned earlier).

Choosing a Training Venue

Sadly, some training centres are only out to make money, and students are left feeling conned, unconfident, and afraid of stepping out into the real (and ruthless) world of commercial grooming. Ultimately, it's the dogs who suffer, in my opinion.

I've always believed that good businesses are built on strong foundations. You've got to be doing what you do for the right reasons (because you genuinely love and have passion for it), before you start charging people for it.

When you are passionate about something you care about, you leave behind a legacy. It's not just about the money, and I think you can tell almost instantly whether a person is doing their job for the love of the dogs - or for the love of the dollar.

You might find better value for money investing in a private tutor as part of an intimate working salon. The benefits of this approach are that you are able to work closely with an experienced groomer and your tuition is catered better to your pace. Some salons offer work placements as bathers, who are given ample opportunity to develop their skills in grooming as an incentive for joining the team.

With bigger training venues, tuition is diluted to cater to more students and it's more likely you will need to attend additional seminars post-training before you really feel confident enough to set out on your own. The environment of a multi-training venue is also a lot more stressful due to the demands being significantly higher.

Research is key.

How to make Multi-Training Establishments Better

There are a few things (based on my own observations and experience) that I would suggest to help make the experience within a busy training centre more positive for all, including:

- Providing students with carefully desensitised dogs for in-house training purposes.
- Hiring more tutors and working with ratios similar to children at nursery. For example, one tutor per two or three students.
- Designated days for learning demonstrations conducted by experienced groomers (and tutors) - limited to small groups of three and four.
- More time to practice styling and tool technique using synthetic model dogs both at home, and during training.
- Practical placements at local shelters, solely for observation and handling opportunities of more 'difficult' dogs under the close supervision of a trained and qualified (positive) behaviourist.
- Starter kits being made available at the beginning of a course - not the end. This allows the student to have the equipment needed to do their practical assignments without having to wait for another student to finish.
- First Aid, Behaviour and Handling courses *before* any practical tuition takes place. This allows the student to be aware of the basics in canine communication techniques prior to any practical thus instilling a degree of confidence from the very beginning.

- Privacy screens between grooming tables to help separate dogs, and prevent distractions during grooms.
- A separate entry, and exit door to avoid dogs meeting face-to-face, and prevent cross-contamination.
- Holding pens, rather than crates for easy access to fresh water, additional comfort, and freedom of movement.
- Toileting areas (either indoor grass zone, or a designated and secure outside doggy space).

You Can't Put A Price On Integrity

True Story

I wrote SIX "first draft" versions of this very book before I felt it was ready to be sent Jo - my 'cut-the-crap' Editor. I then sent the "final" draft to my publishing guru a further THREE times!

The fear of writing a rubbish book, getting something wrong, offending someone with my content, or coming across offensive and/or disrespectful meant I kept re-reading, and re-editing how the words were structured. It was so incredibly stressful.

But I knew that writing this book was the right thing to do, because I cared, and it mattered so much to me.

My point is, when you are choosing a place to study, a mentor, or even a groomer for your dog (if you are a guardian reading this) – whatever the purpose - go with the professional who has a clear love of what they do, who cares about the standard they are providing and who is totally transparent with you from day one.

The person who cannot hide their love for their job is a person worth paying attention to.

Then once you think you have found that person, it's time to dip your toes in.

Asking Questions

If you can take away anything at all from this book it should be this:

- ASK QUESTIONS
- ASK WHEN YOU DON'T UNDERSTAND
- AND MAKE SURE YOU'RE ASKING THE *RIGHT* QUESTIONS

This is your right as a paying and invested student, and it's your tutor's duty to welcome them all. The next step is to really think about the answers and responses you receive. You won't agree with everything your tutor says, and you may have to make your own mind up, but keep asking anyway because it's important to understand the reasons behind why you're being taught a certain technique.

> *"Take the information that resonates with you and disregard the rest."*
>
> — LES BROWN

My tutor was barely around to answer questions, and when she was, many of them would simply ricochet – be wary of the teacher who wants to dictate your education. You are paying to feel confident, and competent therefore, anything less than that is failing to reach your full potential.

Rosettes And Trophies Aren't Everything

Many of us believe that certificates, trophies and rosettes mean that a person is right, when that's not always the case. Don't let the intimidation of a person's success get in the way of your education. It's *your* education for a reason.

And remember, education will evolve as science evolves, so it's not acceptable to be taught a curriculum that's not regularly updated. Ensuring that your mentors, tutors, and education providers are continually investing in their own education is important. If they can't invest in *their* future, why should you invest in them?

I'm going to say something now that could potentially get a few hackles up but... a person who has 20-years of experience might not be teaching appropriately or effectively if the curriculum they still teach is from 20 years ago. If you think about it, you know I'm right. Don't disregard a less experienced groomer too quickly. They will likely be much more up-to-date and eager to go the extra mile for you (I personally know some amazing stylists who have only been in the industry a few short years, who don't happen to have a qualification either!).

Look for a teacher who is *up-to-date* on *up-to-date* methods. Experience and qualifications are good, but the right approach is better and you don't have to be a great stylist to be a great teacher. Due diligence is YOUR responsibility, and yours alone.

Top Tips to Take Away:

- Choose a tutor who you resonate with – their values must reflect your own.
- Choose a tutor who invests in her own education – the evergreen student.
- Choose a tutor who offers one-to-one tuition – quality over quantity (every time).
- Choose a tutor who is passionate – a genuine love for the job reflects on the entire experience.

Note to GUARDIANS: And all of the above applies when choosing the perfect groomer for your beloved pooch too.

Avoid **The Cookie Cutter Approach**

While it may be time efficient to systematically dry a dog a certain way, style a dog to his Breed Standard, or trim his nails before a bath for example, we have to consider his tolerances ahead of our business operations.

> *What does he fear the most?*
> *What makes him feel comfortable?*
> *What do we need to get done as a matter of welfare?*

As I've mentioned, the majority of students are taught how to groom efficiently to make good time, and less how to groom efficiently to reduce stress. The risk in having a systematic process in place for grooming is that you could potentially cause a dog distress very early on, thus resulting in the termination of a groom before the process has even started!

Remember: each dog must be assessed as an individual, and a care plan (of sorts) needs to be devised to cater to their individual needs. Dr Isla Fishburn mentioned why starting with the feet is a bad idea in the Foreword, remember.

And the only exception to this rule applies to welfare cases.

Mini Glossary

WELFARE – the term used to describe dogs requiring immediate attention to prevent further suffering. Examples include: excessive matting, severe skin disorders, parasite infestations, punctured pads due to excessive nail length etc.

EXAMPLE:

Reasonable force, or the use of a muzzle may be required to enable the groomer to cut an overgrown nail that is puncturing the pad.

It is also important to remember that in the instances where a dog is also suffering extreme fear, anxiety and/or stress caused by trauma, it may be kinder to refer him for a sedated clip off at the local Veterinary Surgery. While this is not ideal, it can often be the lesser of two evils. The Holistic Groomer will be confident in carefully evaluating whether a dog requires this approach or not.

Case Study

Toby has 'Tap-Dancing Syndrome' (he really hates his paws being touched, after a bad dew claw injury in the past). He doesn't like going to the grooming salon and is already a little anxious when he arrives.

His guardian requests a full groom, including nail trim.

The groomer decides to trim Toby's nails before the bath. She was told by her tutor that this is the best/only way to do it should she accidently cut the quick and have to wash any blood away. But, as soon as she lifts Toby's paw, all hell breaks loose and his cup (where he metaphorically keeps his emotions) goes from quarter full to overflowing in a matter of moments.

Toby is now too stressed to proceed with anything else, and so the groomer can either send him home, or decide to press on through the groom and increase the risk of a fight response (a bite) in an already very stressful situation.

The groomer decides to press on through. She doesn't want to disappoint the guardian, who is expecting to collect a freshly groomed dog within the hour. The rest of the hour is going to be uncomfortable for everyone!

In order to get the groom done without getting bitten or scratched, the groomer puts a muzzle on Toby, and with the aid of the Groomer's Helper is able to get the groom - including the nail trim - completed on time.

Although the groom was completed 'successfully', the issue with this approach is that the experience has reinforced to Toby that grooming is scary and stressful.

Going forward, Toby will have a negative association with the grooming salon, which will no doubt result in the escalation of behaviours at a much quicker rate. For example, he might become overly distressed upon first entering the salon – or even leaving the house to go there.

A holistic approach can help us to adapt our approach with the needs of each dog in mind.

So, with Toby, rather than start with the nails (if nail trimming is his only fear), we can do everything else first, and end the session with some positive training techniques towards nail-trimming to help him overcome his fear.

This way, we can prevent a traumatic event from ensuing by stopping the appointment at the first sign of distress, without worrying that we are sending the rest of him home 'incomplete' to a disappointed customer.

Choosing The Perfect Groomer

Countless guardians have asked me what to look out for when choosing the perfect groomer for their pet, and it's such a personal question because it really depends on your pet's specific needs and the guardian's expectations.

It's so important that a guardian is realistic with their dog's requirements based on history, lifestyle, medical and health condition, and temperament.

When deciding what to go for, start by asking the following questions:

1. Do I *need* an easy-to-maintain style?
2. Do I *want* a Breed Standard trim?
3. Does my dog suffer anxiety?
4. Is my dog confident and resilient?
5. Can my dog be housed alongside other animals?
6. Does my dog require a one-to-one service?
7. Do I agree with the holistic approach?
8. What do I expect?

The answers to these questions will determine who you choose to work with for the obvious reasons: all groomers operate and specialise in different areas.

True Story

I received an inquiry from a lady who used to come to me with her late Irish Setter who had sadly passed away. They had decided to welcome a new show Cocker Spaniel puppy to their home who was ready for his first "big boy" show-groom. I received an appointment request to get this gorgeous pup booked in as soon as possible.

But I knew I wasn't the best fit for him.

Instead, I referred them on to a lovely groomer nearby who is more talented in show-grooms than I am. I knew she would be able to fulfil their expectations perfectly, and I explained to the dog guardian the reasons for my decision (my speciality is helping anxious dogs find confidence in grooming, and show-styling is not a strong point!).

The lady was so thankful that I was honest with her, and it felt good providing another groomer with a lovely life-long client. It's important that guardians are transparent with their expectations and equally, that groomers are prepared to pass on customers if they think they aren't the best option for a particular dog.

5

LEGISLATION AND THE LAW

"If the law is unjust, a man is not only right to disobey it, he is obligated to do so."

— THOMAS JEFFERSON

Part One – The Flaws In Our Justice System

WHAT STARTED OUT AS A SUBSECTION IN A PREVIOUS CHAPTER has now evolved into a chapter in itself.

Why? Because our justice system is seriously outdated and needs to take responsibility for the countless injustices that happen every single day.

While some of our legislations are in place to protect the quality of care our precious animals receive, there are still a few that do the very opposite.

I want to dedicate this Chapter to the hundreds of families who have suffered at the hands of the authorities who enforce laws that do nothing to protect our dogs, and everything to "destroy" them (LITERALLY).

The Dangerous Dog Act 1991 (Amended 2014)

We are vaguely taught about Legislation and the Law during the theory aspect of our training, but are never encouraged to have anything more than a basic understanding of what they involve. But what I've discovered is our own words, and actions are the real danger in our society.

The Dangerous Dog Act states that it is illegal to own certain types of dog, and hybrids of those breeds.

The banned breeds include the following:

- Pit Bull Terrier
- Japanese Tosa

- Dogo Argentino
- Fifa Brasileiro

A dog can be seized, and destroyed for falling into one of those breeds, irrespective of his temperament. Furthermore, any dog that fits the description of any of the above breeds may also be seized, contained, deported and/or destroyed should the Court decide.

If any dog is deemed "out of control", whether in public or on private property, an authorised dog warden and/or officer may also seize the dog, and keep the dog contained without visitations pending a court case (this can take months, even years).

The Dangerous Dog Act states that all dogs (regardless of breed) should be under "proper control" in a public and/or private place/household.

If a guardian wins their case, they may be granted an exemption certificate for the ownership of the dog, under strict rules. These rules, if breached at any point, will revoke the guardian's rights immediately and result in the deportation, or destruction of the dog.

The important thing to note is that an 'exempt' dog doesn't necessarily mean that the dog is safe...

Skye The Staffordshire Bull Terrier Cross
True Story

Skye The Staffordshire Bull Terrier Cross
(Permission to use image by Skye's Guardian, Chelsea Martin).

Hi Everyone,

My name is Skye. I am 2 years old. When I was just 7 months old, I was taken away from my mummy and sent to police kennels. I was gone for so long, 6 months, locked away, alone and scared. I was not allowed any visits from my family which made me very sad. My mummy had to fight very hard in court to convince the judge to let me come back home. I was not a bad dog. I was just a baby.

She won and I got to go home right in time for Christmas.

Now I am an "exempt" dog, I have to live my life with strict conditions. Mummy needs special insurance for me and I need to wear a muzzle and lead at all times in public – even mummy's car!

Two months after coming home, I heard a loud noise at the door. It was the same people who took me away before. My mummy was crying and screaming. I didn't know what was happening. Mummy went to get my lead but I didn't go for walkies – I went straight in the back of that same van. They had taken me again. Why? I hadn't done anything but love my family. I hadn't hurt anyone. I don't scare anyone. Why did they keep taking me away? Why do they want to kill me?

I spent another 6 months in these cold kennels. Mummy had to fight even harder this time – a nasty neighbour had said I was never on my lead or muzzle, I was "out of control" and they were scared I was going to hurt my humans' babies. I would never do that.

My amazing mummy tried everything to get me home, and eventually the case was dismissed because the nasty liar did not show up at any court dates.

I had spent 12 months in police kennels before I was even 2 years old.

It is now January 2021, and once again Skye has been seized by the local authorities under false accusations that her guardian has failed to adhere to the rules of her exemption.

Proving that both an exemption, and dismissal at court means absolutely nothing, and a dog is never safe.

To join Skye's fight for freedom, you can follow, and support her and her family on Facebook:

'Reach for the Skye to end BSL'.

Breed Specific Legislation (BSL)

If a dog appears to look like one of the banned breeds, or a mix of banned breeds, then it is advised that a member of the public and/or pet professional reports them to the appropriate authorities straight away.

What many behaviour experts find worrying about this legislation however, is that we are encouraged to judge a dog on how he looks, rather than who he is!

Are all handsome male psychology students serial killers? (Ted Bundy, for those who don't watch crime documentaries/binge on Netflix). I rest my case.

And the list of dog breeds we stereotype as automatically "dangerous" keeps growing, and growing, and growing...

Dogs like Staffordshire Bull Terrier's, Mastiff's (of any kind), Akita's, Chow Chow's and any other large, and impressive looking breeds are all being misjudged every single day because:

- The majority of people choose not to understand how to speak dog.
- There are too many irresponsible breeders out there looking to make a quick-buck with little regard for the welfare or wellness of their animals.
- Many dogs are being sold to people who simply do not deserve their companionship (dog-fighting enthusiasts for example).

The ugly truth is that the labelling of breeds is down to nothing more than our ignorance. But I'm hoping that this book will help us to address these issues sooner rather than later.

My advice is, rather than be misguided by the prejudicial influence of some of our more outdated legislations, make a conscious decision to step away from labels and stereotypes (yes, right now), and instead try and read between the lines.

We can ask ourselves:

What makes a dog dangerous?

What does "dangerous" and "out of control" really mean?

What do we now do with the facts we have now uncovered?

How can we help raise awareness of the injustice of these laws?

It all comes down to making responsible decisions based on what we know today – no dog deserves to be punished for merely displaying normal behaviours (barking at a stranger in the garden does NOT mean the dog is "dangerous"), nor do they deserve to be put to sleep because we don't choose to understand them.

Our *Ignorance* Is Life-Threatening

What we are told defines dangerous behaviour, and what we consider a dangerous dog to look like can ultimately lead to the destruction of that dog, if we are not careful.

Yes – our ability to successfully observe is actually a matter of life and death. Additionally, failing to pick up on behaviours early on can result in a dog bite, which again can lead to the destruction of that dog. It is all relevant.

Tyson the Identified Pitbull-Type Breed
True Story

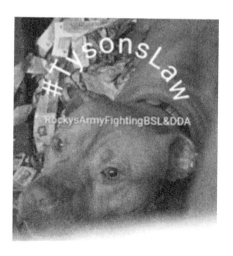

Image taken from Rocky's Army Facebook

My name is Tyson, and I was seized on 17th May 2017 after being identified as a "Pitbull-type breed" by police – I was ten months old.

My 17-year-old human sibling was the only person with me that day when five strangers entered our home. I barked to tell them to leave, before being placed in the garden by my sibling, where she thought I'd be safe.

But I had to protect my family, so I got back inside and barked for them to leave again. They sprayed me with Bite Back spray to try and stop me but I stayed strong – it was my job to keep my home safe. Then the Animal Control Shield came out, but the electrical current reacted with the butane that had been sprayed on my body, and suddenly I was on fire.

I was in so much pain as they tried to put the fire out. I was screaming, and hysterical.

Why did they do this to me? I had done nothing wrong.

They took me away, and confined me in a small kennel and run for 18 months.

The fire placed me in a permanent 'flight' state, and I would do all I could to keep the bad humans away from me.

I heard them call me "aggressive" - I was only trying to keep myself safe!

I lost my faith in humans.
I was numb, broken, in pain, afraid, and defeated.

They never let me see a Vet – my wounds festered.
They never let me see a behaviourist – my trauma escalated.
I was alone, and scared.

And then one day, it went dark.

And I was suffering no more.

On the 16th November 2018, Tyson was given a destruction order at court, and put to sleep in December 2018. The police confirmed that Tyson had never had any complaints against him for behaviour or welfare, nor had the family been brought to their attention.

Tyson was returned to his devastated family in a memorial box, six weeks after he was put to sleep.

Tyson was someone's beloved pet, someone's trusted companion, and someone's entire world!

Control of Dogs (Scotland) Act 2010

I have had first-hand experience of the stress involved in trying to keep my dogs safe, and I want to take this moment to express just how emotionally, physically, and psychologically demanding it is to be subjected to threats when it comes to your animals.

.   .   .

TRUE STORY

Not long after moving into our first bought home, my partner and I received an anonymous handwritten letter through the door, threatening to take us and our two Tibetan Mastiffs to court because they were "out of control". In short? They barked a lot when we were at work, which was unknown to us as we weren't there. Obviously.

Immediately, I sent a letter of response and posted it through every door in the surrounding streets, explaining that we didn't realise and that our dogs barked a lot during our short absences, and that we would try and make things better. I apologised, of course. I added that I would appreciate it if the mystery person would come by the house to talk things over as adults.

Over the next few months, we would often come home to find our back gate wide open, or bits of cooked bone and even things like broken glass thrown into our garden where our dogs would be let out throughout the day. Unfortunately, I had no concrete evidence to suggest any of our neighbours were to blame, so I was forced to let it go.

A few months of this upset continued and passed before we received yet another letter through the door by (presumably owing to the writing) a different neighbour. I was accused of neglecting my dogs, neglecting my children because of my dogs, and being the cause of sleep deprivation for half the county. What an achievement!

In that moment (just weeks after the birth of our second son), I found myself having a full-blown, ugly-crying, mental breakdown at the local doctor's surgery. Almost two years (two bloody years!) without my medication for my mental health conditions that had manifested as a child, and suddenly I was back on them at double my usual dosage.

The truth is, my neighbours didn't like the *look* of my dogs, and whilst I can appreciate how some people may be less comfortable around Tibetan Mastiffs than I am, I didn't appreciate the way I was being treated considering I had only ever tried to resolve their 'neighbourly' concerns in the first place.

Was the fact that my dogs barked occasionally really a good enough reason to subject a young, working family – new to the estate - to such hostility? Well, as it turns out, YES…

Not only do we have to worry about breeds specifically, but any dog – whether he is a Great Dane, Mastiff, or Chihuahua can be seized under these laws also.

Any dog that causes a person to feel threatened, can be deemed "out of control". In the words of the legislation itself, if a person has "reasonable apprehension" that a dog might harm them, the authorities can seize him.

Wait, what?

Yep!

And barking excessively is deemed as out of control – shout out to all of the yappy terriers with "wee man syndrome" (yes, I deliberately stereotyped there!).

It states that all dogs must be under the control of their guardians at all times – even whilst in their own garden!

What's all the more terrifying is that a dog cannot attack a stranger trespassing on private property (a garden, or front lawn) UNLESS the intruder has broken-in, and is physically *inside* the property home.

When discussing the Act, the SSPCA stated, *"Little or no training has been given to local authority staff that have been tasked to carry out this function, and there have been several incidents where the enforcer could not even properly identify the breed of dog or recognise simple dog behavioural traits."*[1]

Bruce The *Suspected* Pit Bull-Type Terrier
True Story

Bruce the suspected Pit Bull-Type Terrier
It was September 19th 2007 when I was seized by local authorities as a banned breed – Pitbull mixes are illegal in Northern Ireland. My life began lonely and sad – I was a stray

puppy with no home. But then I found a loving family to call my own. I spent five years of my life being loved by my rescuers – I was allowed to sleep in my human's bed every night.

But all of that would be a distant memory when the bad humans came.

Suddenly I was locked away in cold, uncomfortable kennels, in a place called Antrim. I had no company, no chance to play or be a dog. I was fed very little and I was so afraid that I tried to escape many times. I hurt myself, and my sores became badly infected but I received no Veterinary care while the council had me secured. My kennel had no comforters, no bedding, and no fresh water. I had sores on my legs from lying on cold concrete every day and I had to have my tail amputated too. When my human was finally allowed to see me, she got a Vet to check me over. She said the council kept telling her she couldn't see me. Why?

After three agonising years of fighting, and barely surviving, my human won the case and was told she could take me home but only if I could get insurance. But nobody would insure a Pitbull-looking breed in Northern Ireland.

I was sent to a rescue in Southern Ireland where I could live out the rest of my days – it was my life, for a life sentence. The lady there called me her "money maker" because I was famous. Everyone wanted to help me so they sent her money to pay for my food and upkeep. But eventually people began to forget about me and the money stopped. The lady kept me tied to a chain all day after that. Years after I arrived at the rescue, the lady was prosecuted for neglect, and other things.

Bruce lived out the rest of his days in a place he could never call home. His family were left devastated and powerless. After three agonising years of fighting for his freedom, he was gifted his right to live, but at a heart-shattering cost.

To summarise my thoughts, what I find so terrifying about The Dangerous Dog Act 1991 (Amended 2014), BSL, and the Control of Dogs (Scotland) Act 2010, is that anyone can report a dog as "out of control" and/or "dangerous".

Which means anyone with a vendetta against you, your family, or your dog has the power to do so much harm. While I'm not saying that these laws can't help to keep our communities safe (when they are dealing with dogs who really cannot be helped), the majority of cases do not see a fair trial, and most families are left heart-broken.

Whichever dog pads his way into your salon (or life), it's important that you know the difference between 'caution with confidence', and 'stereotyping with fear'.

Learning more about canine behaviour and communication develops our compassion as handlers, and suddenly "Fifi the ankle-biter" next door, or the "devil" dog you dread every 6-weeks becomes the dog you look forward to learning from with an open-heart.

Remember: there's no such thing as a bad breed, just bad breeding. There's no such thing as a bad dog, just a bad situation.

And every dog deserves to be understood.

I want to take this moment to dedicate this chapter to all of the dogs who have, and continue to be victims to these legislations, and to their families who are left broken, shattered and traumatised as a result.

I would also like to thank Mark Riley of '**Rocky's Army**' (https://www.facebook.com/groups/209258983148253).

And to Jayne Dendle, of '**Save Our Seized Dogs**' (https://www.facebook.com/PBSLTSUK).

Your relentless efforts to help bring hope and change to an industry that's failing many dogs across the UK is truly an inspiration.

If you would like to help improve our failing system, you can sign "A Call To Parliament To Pass A Law For Better Welfare Standards for Care of Seized Dogs", here: http://chng.it/f2TqtzfZrX.

Part Two – Animal Welfare

"Until we extend our circle of compassion to all living things, humanity will not find peace."

— ALBERT SCHWEITZER

It seems more important than ever to protect the welfare of all dogs (and animals), after reading the stories of but a few of the victims of our unjust system.

But what I found most astonishing was the blatant breach of another of our animal specific laws (specifically The Animal Welfare Act 2006) by the very law-enforcers who attempt to fulfil the duty of keeping our society free from dangerous dogs (and I use the term dangerous very loosely)!

All seized dogs are deprived of even the most basic of animal needs – if that isn't hypocritical, I don't know what is. Let's take a closer look...

Animal Welfare Act 2006

It's worthwhile that we all take the time to read through the Animal Welfare Act 2006 before thinking about getting involved in caring for an animal (see Resources for a link).

In brief, the Act states that anyone responsible for an animal must ensure that they are taking the reasonable steps to ensure the animal's specific needs are being met, and reminds us that we have a "duty of care" in doing this.

The Act contains laws relating to Animal Welfare and notes that **it is an offence to cause any unnecessary suffering to an animal**.

The problem with this Act however (and many others), is that many of us fail to take the time to understand what "unnecessary suffering" means to an animal, and how to demonstrate best practice.

Instead, many of us try to justify certain methods and/or practices of working with animals as necessary measures of "getting the job done", not realising that many of the methods we see are outdated and disproved (Dominance theory to name but one).

This is why furthering our education in up-to-date practice is so crucial.

The Five Freedoms

Part of the Animal Welfare Act 2006 includes 'The Five Freedoms' which have been used as a reliable benchmark for devising animal care protocols in most animal businesses across the globe since they were first introduced by Roger Brambell and his committee in 1965. This breakthrough in animal welfare occurred after the publication of a provocative book called '*Animal Machines*' by Ruth Harrison in 1964 that exposed the flaws of farming practice in Britain, which forced the Government to investigate the agriculture industry.

The Five Freedoms are as follows:

Freedom from hunger and thirst
- providing ready access to fresh water and a diet to maintain full health and vigour.

Freedom from discomfort
- providing an appropriate environment including shelter and a comfortable resting area.

Freedom from Pain, Injury and Disease

- prevention or rapid diagnosis and treatment of illness and injury.

Freedom to express normal behaviour

- providing sufficient space, proper facilities and company of the animal's own kind.

Freedom from fear and distress

- ensuring conditions and/or treatment that avoids mental suffering.

While they have an important role to play, it's important that both guardians and professionals learn to understand the true purpose of the freedoms and avoid taking them too literally, or too vaguely.

For one, we must remember that it is not possible, nor healthy for an animal to be totally "free" from stress. But additionally, it's simply not ok to deprive an animal of constant access to fresh water, especially when in the grooming environment (something I have sadly seen happen one too many times).

A Holistic Groomer can opt to use a more recent adaption of the five F's called, the 'Five Domains', which were introduced by Professor David Mellor and Dr Cam Reid in 1994.

THE FIVE DOMAINS

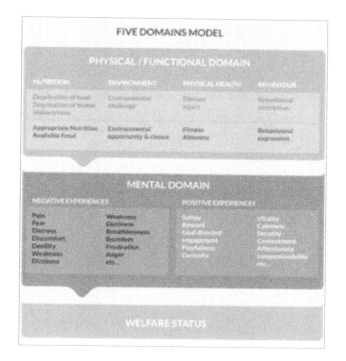

Figure 1 taken from Wild Welfare Website (see referenes).

The purpose of the Five Domains model (Figure One) was to instead identify and grade the welfare of animals, and so the statements are formed in a way that is less receptive to misinterpretation.

The first four domains represent the biological functions, and physical wellbeing of the animal, and the fifth considers the 'affective state' or psychological wellbeing of the animal, and his overall subjective feelings and/or experiences – the fifth domain is the key element of animal welfare[2,3].

The domain terms allow for a clear distinction between the physical and functional factors that affect an animal's welfare. The benefits of using the Five Domains in Holistic Grooming (and in other animal care professions), is that they recognise the significance that each of the four physical aspects has on the mental state of the animal (whether it is positive or negative). Why this is so important will be explained later chapters.

Mellor and Reid understand that when it comes to safeguarding the health, wellbeing and welfare of an animal, his emotional needs are equally as important as his physical needs, and that an animal requires more than just the removal from a negative physical and/or mental state in order to be fully content. The purpose of the Five Domains model is to provide animals with opportunities to experience positive emotions by providing them with enrichment to suit their functional characters.[4]

We can certainly use this to adapt our approach and our environment in the salon by introducing ways to enrich the dogs in our care, based on their individual needs and functional characteristics.

Veterinary Surgeons Act 1966 (VSA)

In short, only a qualified Veterinarian can offer professional advice on the treatment of animals.

All pet professionals should be qualified and, as such, authorised to perform emergency first aid on an animal in an attempt to alleviate suffering, prevent a condition from worsening and/or save a life.

Many Holistic Groomers might choose to venture off into alternative therapies such as Bach's Flower Remedies, Reiki, Crystal Healing, or Animal Communication, and that's great, but again, only a Vet can offer professional advice on the medical care of an animal.

Additionally, it's important you receive the appropriate training and certification to perform any alternative therapies as part of your professional practice, and also request the written permission from both the animal's registered Vet and guardian prior to any appointments.

In fact, there are many Holistic Vets now implementing alternative therapies into their practice, alongside conventional medicine, which is great news for our precious pets!

The Microchipping of Dogs (England) Act 2015 (and Scotland, 2016)

All dogs are required to be microchipped by law before they reach 8 weeks of age, unless otherwise deemed unfit (sick, low body weight, etc) by a Veterinarian. A certificate must be issued to the breeder or guardian to confirm this.

The purpose of a microchip is to prove guardianship of an animal, and to reunite lost and/or stolen animals with their families. Yet, between 2018 and 2019, 69,621 stray or abandoned dogs were taken to rescue shelters in the UK. Only 54% of these were reunited with their guardians. An estimated 24% were passed to a welfare organisation, with an estimated 1,303 dogs being euthanised; 137 due to ill health, 198 due to behavioural problems, 48 under the Dangerous Dogs Act, and 39 due to being unclaimed (or having no rescue centres available to take them). Furthermore, 38% of stray dogs brought in during that time were indeed microchipped, but 79% of those were unable to be reunited with their families due to incorrect contact details.[5] Please, update your details if you have a microchipped pet.

Since the puppy boom of lockdown (the first one – March 2020), there has been an increase of dog thefts throughout the world, meaning that it's more important than ever to raise awareness of microchipping - and the importance of updating details. As groomers, we can prompt our clients to check their microchip details regularly to help do our bit to reduce these harrowing stats in future years.

Additionally, many missing pets are never found because microchip scanning is not a necessary routine procedure at Vets surgeries or other professional settings, though it really should be.

Chips can often migrate to other parts of the body, which needs to be reported to the appropriate authorities via a Microchip Adverse Event form. When an animal is registered missing, the national database that the chip is registered to will put an alert on the implanted chip within the dog that will give off a signal to the scanner when scanned, which will in turn alert the handler that the pet has been reported missing.

But why is this relevant in grooming?

If all pet professionals were encouraged to invest in a microchip scanner, more dogs would be reunited with their families, I'm certain. And maybe in a future edition of this book, I won't have to report such shocking stats.

6

THE SCIENCE OF EMOTIONS AND BEHAVIOUR

"Animals do speak, but only to those who know how to listen."

— ORHAN PAMUK

BEFORE WE EVEN THINK ABOUT BEHAVIOUR, WE NEED TO understand what behaviour is, and why an animal might act a certain way. When we look at how we ourselves are made and how this is relevant when we are observing the world around us, we become more aware of how we approach every individual encounter with a dog.

Equally, our relationship with our family pet will also be nurtured as we learn better ways of communication that will bring harmony to our home environments too. This chapter is dedicated to a friend, and mentor of mine who continues to amaze me with her teachings every day.

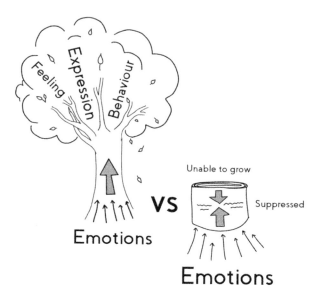

Part One – Biochemistry, Cells, Energy and Emotions

"Re-examine all you have been told. Dismiss what insults your soul."

— WATT WHITMAN

The Relevance of Biochemistry

Dr. Isla Fishburn (who is arguably one of the smartest and most inspiring women I have ever met, by the way) teaches her students about biochemistry, the relevance of epigenetics, and the wonders of genomes when it comes to understanding our dogs - and ourselves - a whole lot better.

Since starting her course, 'Canine Wellness', I have discovered many unbelievable facts that further explain why humans and canines have been able to co-exist so harmoniously up until this point, and I continue to be blown away the more I learn as her student.

Discoveries in biochemistry have at last verified what many strange, and wonderful people have often speculated (what if we are all connected on a subliminal level? What if hugging trees could cure disease?). In fact, indigenous tribes have been teaching us about the wonders of Mother Nature and natural healing for hundreds of years but it's only recently science is now revealing that they have been right all along (there goes the "hippy nonsense" stereotype - yay!).

When we learn more about our very *'beings'*, things like behaviour and emotions seem to just fall into place. Suddenly, we are more compassionate to others and we are more open-minded to the idea that some things really do require a less is more approach.

If you've ever seen the movie 'Avatar' then you may just have an idea of how this is possible (if you haven't, I suggest you do).

What Is An Ecosystem?

A dog - and every other living/non-living thing in our world - is an ecosystem; made up of cells and energy, whereby each part is constantly communicating and interacting with their internal and external environments. An ecosystem is incredibly sensitive to its environment and relies on safety to be balanced, happy, and healthy. When our ecosystem (our very being) is exposed to suffering, there is a disruption in our energy flow that results in a physical, emotional and often, physiological reaction. Furthermore, when an animal is faced with prolonged exposure to suffering, the immune and digestive system also suffers, and chronic illnesses ensue. [1]

The definition of an ecosystem is as follows:

> *"A complex network of interconnected systems, which emphasise the interaction between living and non-living parts and the flow of materials and energy between these parts."*

> — CHAMBERS DICTIONARY OF SCIENCE AND
> TECHNOLOGY

What Is Emotion and How Does It Work?

Emotion is energy, or rather, energy in motion. And emotions? They're what our body creates in response to any given thing that we are surrounded by – our environment, our relationships, our own health… they are all influencers that cause a cellular reaction resulting in an emotional response.

Both the heart and the brain generate vibrational frequencies carrying our thoughts, feelings and emotions from one place to another. These electromagnetic frequencies have the ability to transfer over or out the individual; and thus, be received by another individual.

The word 'emotion' derives from the Latin 'emotere' meaning *"energy in motion"*, which suggests that emotions are meant to flow[2]. Emotions should be felt, experienced and released by a recipient to enable that person to learn and grow stronger and more resilient with their inner and outer environment.

All living beings have molecules, cells, and energy that pulsates through them. Energy (otherwise known as Electromagnetic Frequencies or 'EMF') is what births emotions and leads to the behaviours we express. Additionally, our cells are constantly, and instantaneously reacting and communicating with everything in their internal and external environments, consciously and subconsciously.

In Dr. Isla's course, we learn that our environment, both internal and external, is what influences the health and wellness of our ecosystem. How a dog behaves therefore, is a reflection of how healthy his ecosystem is, and his behaviour is merely the physical expression that we see of his underlying emotional state.

EXAMPLE:

Harry the Westie is restricted on the grooming table during his groom. When you lift his tail to clip, he begins to snarl,

bite and paw at you. Harry's emotional and/or physical state is compromised due to an imbalance in his ecosystem.

His very biochemistry is disrupted due to an internal and/or external environmental stressor; it could be fear, pain, or an underlying medical condition. His autonomic nervous system has engaged his sympathetic nervous system, which has resulted in an instinctual, physical survival response (what some groomers might call "undesirable behaviours").

He is trying to warn you away and escape from the immediate threat. Since he is restricted, his body decides that the only way to defend himself is to engage the 'fight' response.

The Holistic Groomer can use this knowledge to try and pinpoint what the cause of Harry's behaviour is by adapting parts of their approach by asking themselves the following questions:

What is disrupting the flow of the dog's energy?

Why is he behaving this way?

What can I do to help him feel safer?

Depending on what the cause is, there are many ways we can help to make the overall grooming experience more positive for dogs that require a more bespoke approach. Remember that everything is interconnected, and so when one thing is off balance, it has a domino effect. The holistic approach is to consider the entire context around each situation that's in front of them.

Note: there are some instances where the cause might be completely unknown to the groomer, guardian and other professionals (such as Vets), yet a dog might still be displaying erratic fear, anxiety or stress. This can be a result of genetics, heritage, and/or what is known as 'Transgenerational Trauma'.

What's Transgenerational Trauma, and how is it relevant?

Some psychological and emotional trauma can come from when the animal was within the womb based on how healthy the mother was – we know that an unhealthy and unhappy mother will result in unhealthy, unhappy pups.

But additionally, memory of a certain traumatic event can be deeply integrated into the cells of an animal, and passed down through generations to come! Meaning that some animals can in fact, be influenced by a significant experience/traumatic event of an ancestor!

This event would have been so severe, and such a great risk to the animals' very survival that the memory of the event would be imprinted so deeply into the cells, that it would change the very DNA of that animal's lineage. This would mean that all of the animals predecessors would instinctively know to engage the Sympathetic Nervous System as soon as the particular fear stimulus is presented to him. Evolution is an incredible thing, but it can prove to be problematic when dealing with an animal suffering what we now know as, 'transgenerational trauma'.[3]

Cells store memory and DNA can be altered in an attempt to keep animals safe.

When we are dealing with a phobia as deep-rooted into the dog as transgenerational trauma, there is very little we can do to change it, but that doesn't mean we can't manage it, or come up with an alternative approach that doesn't trigger as big a stress response in that situation.

Case Study

Oisin the Labrador has an extreme phobia of water from a hose, yet his guardians can confirm that there are no known negative experiences with water to explain why he is so afraid of being bathed in this way.

It is more than possible that one of his ancestors was subject to such a traumatic experience with water, meaning that even years later, and despite having never been in a related traumatic situation, even the very sight of water from a hose sends Oisin into the fight-flight response.

After many different and failed attempts to desensitise Oisin to the bathing process of the grooming environment, I began researching alternatives and came across 'Mud Daddy'. Somehow, the low-pressure of this manual pump hose isn't as scary as the pressure from an industrial hose connected to a Hydrobath. Even so, this device had to be carefully and gradually introduced to Oisin at his own pace - using high-value treats and plenty of praise.

This is an example of thinking outside the box and is the reason why it's important to research the available tools on the market for your trade - and be willing to try them out.

Readers can claim their exclusive discount to Dr Isla Fishburn's course (suitable for all dog lovers) via the Resources page.

Human vs Dog Emotions

There's one significant difference between our emotional capabilities compared to those of our dogs that we must know about, and that's our ability to control how we respond to our emotions far more successfully due to our neo-cortex - an area of the brain = being bigger.

This explains why a dog does not intentionally set out to make us angry, but instead acts on an emotional impulse. Dogs, or other non-human animals in fact, cannot lie. They simply exhibit the emotion they are feeling in that moment.

Even so, the similarity between the raw emotional capabilities in both humans and dogs could explain why we have been so successful in living together thus far, and why dogs truly are "man's best friend"[4].

WHAT IS WELLNESS?

When a dog feels safe on all levels, he is generally much healthier.

Wellness really just means when the dog is healthy as a whole - physically, emotionally, physiologically, mentally and spiritually (remember the Five Domains?).

A dog that feels *safe* has less chance of suffering distress, chronic disease and illness. After all, this is what disease is; a dis-ease or dis-stress in the dog's ecosystem.

Health and wellness are dependent on how efficiently our energy is flowing, pulsating and vibrating through our cells ("ours", as in, ALL animals).

When a dog (or other living being) is suffering in one or more of these states, the energy flow is disrupted and we see a range of health conditions and behaviours on display.

"Environmental stress refers to how people and animals respond to physical, chemical and biological features of their environment. Whether one-time or long-term, environmental stressors cause strain on the body and mind. The response of the body ranges from a short-term fight-or-flight response, to long-term changes to your health."[5]

And don't you think that the grooming environment alone just screams RISK to safety?

Can you imagine how much scarier (and stressful) the environment might seem to the dog who has experienced an additional traumatic event in the already scary place?

EXAMPLE:

A two-year-old girl has always looked forward to her mum giving her a mini-manicure. But one day, mum accidently cuts a nail too short, hurts the child, and the blood comes pouring out.

The child freaks out in shock and pain, thinks she is losing a finger, and takes an hour or so to calm down.

And now? Every time those nail trimmers come out, the child is reminded of the one time when mum cut her finger, it hurt, and she nearly bled to death.

All hell breaks loose once more.

It might take the child many months to overcome her fear of those nail trimmers, but with a little bit of patience and some desensitisation, the girl will come around.

Failing such intervention, it'll still be okay, because as her brain develops, so does the child's ability to think logically. Eventually, she will learn to control her fear through careful management of those nail trimmers.

But remember, dogs don't have that luxury…

It's down to the professional/guardian to desensitise and counter-condition dogs to the process all over again, should they hope to be able to overcome their fear. And, the hard reality is that, in some cases, the dog may never be able to overcome the trauma. Trauma, and the ability to overcome it, is specific to each individual.

Part Two – Safety, Behaviour and Expression

"Animals share with us the privilege of having a soul."

— Pythagoras

What is Behaviour?

Behaviour is the consequence of a certain emotional state of an animal, which in dogs is controlled by the Autonomic Nervous System and Endocrine System. When a dog is feeling threatened, he will display an element of expressions in his intent to communicate his fear, anxiety or stress.

Energy frequencies, based on each given moment, are sent to the 'Autonomic Nervous System' which then determines the emotional state of the animal. The ANS connects the brain to mostly all major organs of the body and influences breathing, heart rate and even an animal's digestion.

There are two emotional states of the ANS – 'Sympathetic', and 'Parasympathetic' which reflect either positive or negative (healthy or unhealthy) energy states.

The Sympathetic Nervous System

Dogs have an instinctual need to feel safe and to survive.

When they are exposed to a situation that's unfamiliar, the body (cells, molecules and energy) will make an instinctive decision to prepare the body to react in a certain way.

Once the brain decides that something is a threat, it will send the message to the rest of the dog's body to prepare for a survival response. With the sympathetic system now engaged, the homeostatic regulation of the dog will change and behaviours will begin to surface, including salivating, panting, shivering, shaking, yawning, tension, snarling, whining, barking, biting, lunging and so on.

Depending on the context, a dog will react in whichever way his instincts tell him he needs to react in order to survive – he has no choice, nor an ability to logically think about his actions. What's more, it can take days or even weeks for a dog's autonomic system to go back to parasympathetic mode, and so it is vital that he is able to rest after a particularly stressful event to avoid trigger stacking and sensory overload.[6]

When a dog is exposed to too much stress, he may respond in five ways:

1. Flight (or Flee)
2. Freeze
3. Fight
4. Fool around
5. And also, Faint

It's also important to note that arousal of the positive sort can also lead to the activation of the Sympathetic Nervous System, therefore it is wise to try and limit the number of times your dog is aroused throughout the days and weeks to avoid chronic health conditions from ensuing.

Based on what we now know, isn't it safe to say that dogs react on emotional impulse? Meaning that labels such as "aggressive", "spiteful", and "nasty" are not only wrong but extremely unfair.

ACTIVITY

Repeat After Me:

There is no such thing as a *spiteful* dog.

There is no such thing as a *nasty* dog.

There is no such thing as an *aggressive* dog.

The Parasympathetic Mode

The Parasympathetic state is a calm, relaxed and *safe* state which we should all try to encourage in ourselves and the dogs in our care. This is the healthiest state we can be in and one that promotes health and wellbeing – Holistic Groomers want to try their best to maintain parasympathetic mode throughout the grooming experience.

But don't get too frustrated, grooming can be quite strenuous as we've already covered and we must be mindful that it's often not possible to achieve a completely stress-free experience.

Think about it, we have to harass animals to carry out our roles (it's true)!

Could you imagine being handled at the hairdresser or barbers the way we handle our dogs every day? Just think how many harassment claims we'd be making! People are right in saying that most dogs would never *choose* to visit the groomers. The difference in the holistic approach however, is that we can try to make the ordeal a little less of an ordeal through adapting our approach.

By adapting our environment to help keep our dogs (and in turn, ourselves) as relaxed as possible we could:

- Introduce handling carefully and positively
- Be respectful and gentle when handling your dog
- Be confident and relaxed in your communication
- Observe and listen to the subtle cues the dog is giving off
- Be prepared to provide ample rest, water and toilet breaks frequently throughout the session
- Be ready to adapt your approach based on the dog's changing emotional state
- Be mindful of our own emotions when we are getting restless - take a break if needed.
- Don't give guardians a specific time to collect their dog to remove all urgency

Rule of thumb is:

Fearful dog = less is more, more frequently.

Confident dog = more is more, less frequently.

Meaning don't spend an hour with a dog who is extremely stressed, opt for shorter sessions more frequently to prevent an escalation of behaviours, and keep things as positive and calm as possible. Confident dogs will be more resilient to a typical grooming appointment of between 1.5 and 2.5 hours (depending on breed type, of course).

Observation of Expression

An animal will almost always give off subtle cues to express how he is feeling, before an erratic behaviour ensues. It is down to the handler to be competent in their observation skills and ability to communicate successfully with a dog.

One of the very first places we can observe a disruption to the flow of energy in an animal is on the face and hands/legs, followed by the rest of the body. A disruption of energy (often referred to as suppressed energy) in dogs is predominantly stored in the face and joints of the body – just as it is with humans.

Pay attention to the jaw, mouth, neck and head in particular.

When a dog is feeling uncomfortable, stressed, afraid or anxious he will begin to display subtle 'calming signals' in these areas, that look like:

- Tension in the jaw, curled lip, tongue flicking, grin, yawning, panting and/or drooling
- Turning away, averted gaze, whale eye and/or slow blinking
- Drawn back ears, paw lifting

- Stiffness of body, lowered head, tucked tail
- Frozen stance, curled body, tucking feet, an attempt to appear smaller

Turid Rugaas believes that a dog, like wolves will display the same "cut-off", or more appropriately referred to as "calming signals" to diffuse, and/or avoid conflict.[7]

Failure to recognise these signals results in an escalation (or dramatisation of these behaviours) that many groomers might refer to as, "difficult", "aggressive", or "nuisance" behaviours, such as:

- Pulling, crocodile rolling, jumping, and trying to escape
- Growling, whining, and barking
- Snarling, air snapping, clawing, and biting
- Rolling over, licking excessively, humping, and goofing around
- Sickness, urinating and/or soiling
- Frozen stance, fainting, and seizures

A Breakdown Of 'Undesired' Behaviours

Now that we understand what energy, emotions and behaviours are, we now need to develop our understanding of what they look like and how we can observe them better in the grooming environment.

When groomers and guardians talk about undesired behaviours they typically mean:

- Barking
- Chewing
- Licking
- Humping
- Howling
- Biting
- Scratching
- Whining

When we identify these behaviours as the physical expression of a feeling based on either their internal and/or external environment then we can begin to look at the whole context. Developing our canine and holistic perspective will help us to evaluate and often problem-solve the possible causes by asking ourselves questions like:

WHY is the dog barking?

WHY is the dog growling at me?

WHY does the dog keep urinating on the floor?

WHY does the dog try and bite me when I lift his leg?

What's going on beneath the surface, and how do we resolve this problem?

Apart from hereditary, and genetic issues, it usually comes down to one of three things:

1. Pain/Illness
2. Anxiety/Fear of something
3. Boredom

Process of elimination is a valuable tool in the Holistic Grooming environment to help us pinpoint any potential environmental stressors, but we should also be considering the dog's health and lifestyle too. These are areas which will be covered in the Phone Consultation and initial Meet and Treat appointments with guardians prior to a grooming session.

Environmental Stressors

If we consider that an animal is exposed to constant environmental stressors throughout each day, it becomes an even bigger problem again.

A dog that attends a grooming appointment may already be aroused due to a negative experience prior to their appointment, making the escalation of behaviours more erratic should he be presented with additional stressors within the grooming environment itself.

"The straw to break the camel's back", so to speak.

This disruption of energy results in numerous behaviours we see daily, especially in the grooming environment, where the chances of sensory overload are so very common.

TRIGGER STACKING, Flooding and Desensitisation

Trigger stacking can occur when a series of environmental stressors or other unfamiliar experiences build up over a short period of time, resulting in emotional overload.

Short term, this can result in physical and/or psychological harm to either/both the groomer and the dog, such as a bite, learned helplessness, or emotional shutdown.

Long term, over-exposure of environmental stressors can trigger often serious health conditions, combined with a quicker escalation to the fight response - which results in an increased risk of dog bites.

And so you're already seeing why it's so important for the Holistic Groomer to constantly observe an animal, and for both guardian and groomer to ensure they introduce potentially fearful stimulus through careful desensitisation methods.

Mini Glossary

Desensitisation - when something is introduced to the dog gradually, and at his own pace, always using positive reinforcement. It is a form of operant conditioning that can help to relieve the underlying cause of a dog's discomfort and/or fear in response to a stimulus.

Flooding - often mistaken as desensitisation, over-exposing an animal to his fear, causing him to become more sensitised to the stimulus, often resulting in a survival response and/or the emotional shut-down of an animal.

EXAMPLE

When a dog displays signs of fear while being bathed, but the groomer continues to bath the dog. Eventually, the dog appears to settle down thus causing the groomer to think she has successfully desensitised the dog to the bath.

A Holistic Groomer understands the difference between desensitisation and flooding.

Now that we know a behaviour is merely the physical response to the very biochemistry of an animal at each given point, and that their cells are responding to a certain trigger, it is more effective long term to try and resolve the root of a problem than to try and control the physical behaviour using restraints or outdated training methods.

Understanding that the grooming process can be broken up into smaller and more manageable chunks for the more fearful dog, and leaving the most stressful tasks to the end in order to limit the number of triggers activated throughout the grooming process, are just two ways we can avoid flooding.

Again, there are circumstances where it is impossible to determine a cause (transgenerational trauma or lack of background knowledge in a rescue dog for example), therefore there are times when careful management is the only way to proceed.

Are you now beginning to see a connection throughout each of the different techniques a Holistic Groomer can use? Repetition is unavoidable considering that the approach to Holistic Grooming is all inter-linked.

Everything is connected to everything else.

Part Three – Reducing Fear and Increasing Observation

> *"Humans aren't the only animals trying to survive each day."*

— ANTHONY DOUGLAS WILLIAMS

Fear, Anxiety, Stress (FAS)

In the Fear Free™ protocol, students are taught how to monitor levels of fear, anxiety and/or stress.[8] We can do this through our observation of body language and behaviours – for example, what signals is the dog giving off to suggest that he needs a break?

There's been much stick about "consent-grooming" and "co-operative grooming" lately, when there really doesn't need to be. In simple terms, the terms basically mean that we give a little bit of choice back into the lives of our animals to prevent the escalation of FAS.

Does that mean we need to ask Snoopy if he would like to have his blueberry facial today, or give him the option to leave it this time?

God, I hope not (but there's always one).

Assessing Behaviour

Now that we know energy is emotion, and emotion is expressed in the physical behaviours we see, we can now say that behaviours are emotions in physical form.

Based on the immediate environment (internally, and externally), a dog is constantly displaying behaviours that reflect his emotions, his energy frequency and his overall health and well-being state.

A dog will respond to his environment instinctively, based on his indigenous need to survive and feel safe.

When in doubt, we can use the Five Domains and Marty Becker's FAS Scale to help us assess the current emotional and mental state of a dog. Our duty is to make sure that a dog is never subjected to prolonged stress.

ACTIVITY

Time to get your Bruno on again!

You are Bruno the scaredy-cat-dog, only this time, you have been tied to a table, muzzled and elevated into the air on a platform. Your leg is being yanked and held firmly in place by an unfamiliar person who you can sense is angry with you.

Any time you try to tell this person that you are afraid, they give you a stern "no" and continue doing what they are doing.

Two hours later, you are finally allowed down off the table.

Spend some time really thinking about this activity and take mental notes about how you feel.

How To Help A Dog Feel Safe

I hope it's now obvious to you that safety isn't just about securing the grooming space to prevent an escapee dog from getting out the front door and onto a busy road (heaven forbid)! Safety is also about how safe a dog FEELS in his environment.

When it comes to the grooming procedure, there are a few main reasons why a dog may feel unsafe, including:

- When a dog feels trapped or restricted of movement
- When a dog feels intimidated, under pressure or vulnerable
- When a dog is deprived of rest when tired
- When a dog feels forced to do something that he doesn't want to do

It's time to be honest: how safe would you feel in a commercial grooming environment?

Why should we expect dogs to be any different?

As groomers and guardians, we need to be mindful of the canine perspective and how the dog might be feeling. We need to ask ourselves:

Does the dog (or animal) feel safe right now?

Am I doing enough to make the dog feel confident and comfortable?

Is the dog displaying any signs that he is in distress or discomfort?

What can I do to make the experience better?

How would I feel?

Why Consent-Based Grooming Is Safe

I think it's easy to allow our imagination to run away with us here, but consent-based grooming is about introducing an element of choice in the lives of our animals. It really is that simple.

Choice doesn't need to be complicated at all and we can better understand the significance of choice through examples of choice in our own lives as humans.

EXAMPLE:

It's time for your routine smear/prostate check at the GP.

The letter comes through the post and the dread begins to fester.

You weigh up the pros and cons of attending the appointment, before finally deciding that your health is important and you'll just have to grin and bear it.

The appointment itself is awkward, uncomfortable and nerve-wracking. You feel tense and struggle to relax, but the GP is friendly and helps you to feel *slightly* better.

Within a few minutes, the procedure is over.

Congratulations, you don't have to think about this again for another 3-5 years.

But for dogs... it's not as easy as that!

Remember:

- Dogs don't choose to go to the groomers.
- Dogs can't understand when we tell them to relax, stay calm or stop moving.
- Dogs are expected to endure stress for extended periods of time (and often the whole day when in multi-grooming environments).
- When dogs resist, they are usually restrained further, thus exacerbating the whole stressful experience.

Just as we don't necessarily want to go to the Dentist, a dog won't necessarily want to attend the groomers, but we can introduce choice by learning how to 'speak dog'; picking up on the subtle cues they show us to tell us when they need to rest, for example.

Allowing rest breaks is a great way to introduce choice in the grooming environment, as is adapting our environment itself to suit the specific needs of the dog.

Next time you feel your blood pressure rising when the poodle you have on the table continues to sit as you attempt to scissor the leg, and you decide you're going to tackle him into an additional handling restraint, think:

Is he tired?

Does he need a break?

Can I perhaps work on a different area to allow him to sit a while?

How can I make this less stressful for him, and for myself?

MYTH BUSTER: Additional breaks means more time – not always the case!

Sometimes a dog will cooperate better after having had a couple of moments to stretch his legs, go for a piddle or have a quick game of fetch!

Try it and see what happens. It may surprise you.

Remember: We can make positive and often, instantaneous differences through a series of small changes. All the while, contributing to the dog's sense of wellness and our own.

Why Less Restraints Can Be Safer

I've found that the use of restraints encourages the groomer to observe less. Whilst it's not realistic to have your eyes constantly on a dog whilst using a pair of scissors, it's also not advisable to use restraints as an alternative to observation.

Observation and handling should never be compromised.

Why is this important?

In an earlier chapter I spoke about the flow of energy and why animals need to express emotion freely. Restraints can disrupt the energy flow when not introduced/used properly, so that's something to bear in mind.

Changing our approach to grooming can help keep the dog relaxed - or at least relaxed enough to avoid a traumatic experience from ensuing.

By observing and monitoring the level of stress in the dog during the session, we can provide him with ample rest breaks (and whatever else he needs) to keep him under his threshold.

ACTIVITY

Next time you have a dog in the salon who is panicking on the grooming table, try lowering the table right the way down to floor level and removing all handling restraints. Instead, allow the dog to leave the table every so often and

encourage him back on using high value rewards and praise.

The dog will soon learn not to fear the grooming table and you can begin to introduce grooming gradually using the same positive methods.

It could be that the height of the table is causing the dog to feel unstable, and the restraints are removing a potential "flight" response too – when a dog is particularly fearful of being groomed, he will have a quicker escalation of behaviours if his options are limited, and what's more, a trapped animal is more likely to fight through a threat to keep safe.

Note: for dogs with a bite history, you may wish to proceed with this approach with the help of a guardian and the use of a safety muzzle. Be responsible when working with a dog who has been known to bite people – start slow to build his trust.

There are some medical and genetic conditions that may require a dog to always be muzzled during an appointment, and that's ok. Our job as Holistic Groomers is to ensure that he is comfortable and that muzzles are introduced and used safely using positive reinforcement.

Grooming Contributes To The Bigger Picture Of An Animals Health

Does one grooming appointment every 4, 6, 8 or even 12 weeks really make a difference?

Yes, it does.

Holistic Grooming is all about considering the bigger picture.

Groomers will often see a dog more than any other pet professional (especially as intimately), which means we make more of a difference to the wellbeing of our clients than we think.

We are required to thoroughly examine a dog during the initial health check pre-groom. Guardians and Vets often rely on us being able to identify early signs of illness and/or injury, therefore dedicating time to building a dog's confidence to being handled within the grooming setting can make all the difference long term to the overall health, and wellbeing of the dog.

We must be mindful of the influence we have on a dog's physical, physiological, psychological, emotional, and spiritual state, if we don't, we can contribute to the cause of many chronic illnesses that we see in our animals today.

Sounds dramatic, but it's true.

In Summary:

- Experiences are remembered and stored in the cells.
- A negative experience is stored longer, stronger and faster than a positive one.
- When a dog is highly aroused, behaviours can escalate at a faster rate – leading to the activation of the sympathetic system and the four Fs (freeze, flee, fight, fool around).
- It's harder to resolve a learned fear - especially fear caused by a significant traumatic event.
- When the nervous system is in a constant state of arousal, the digestive and immune systems are also disrupted, and illness ensues.

- Repeated activation of the stress response takes its toll on the body – resulting in high blood pressure, blood clots, and chemical imbalances in the brain, resulting in chronic anxiety, stress and depression.
- It can take weeks for the body to return to parasympathetic mode after a stressful event – therefore, any additional environmental stressors within this time frame following the grooming appointment can further escalate behaviours, resulting in sensory overload.
- Avoid making/booking grooming appointments on the same week as other stressful appointments and/or events, e.g. – visits to the Vet, the immediate aftermath of an injury, or a stay in the kennels if the guardians are going on holiday.

Part Four – Our Universal Connection

"All things share the same breath – the beast, the tree, the man - the air shares its spirit with all the life it supports."

— CHIEF SEATTLE

Feeling Energy

I believe the very atmosphere of our environment is picked up by more than the five senses, and developing our spiritual awareness is part of the journey in holistic care.

TRUE STORY

When I was a child, my parents took my sister and I on a road trip 'up North'.

I will never forget the sudden sense of fear I had as we passed a specific part of the Scottish Highlands, and I pleaded with my dad to get us out of the place as fast as possible. I couldn't stop shaking. My body was tingling like the onset of pins and needles.

I remember my parents looked shocked at my reaction, but it wasn't until years later that I discovered why that had happened.

It turns out, my reaction came just as we drove through Glencoe.

The area we drove through bears the dark history we know today as the 'Massacre of Glencoe'. Look it up, if you get the chance. Despite the horrific event taking place hundreds of years earlier, I felt something. And I didn't like it.

Researchers have discovered that humans pick up on chemo-signals left through sweat and/or tears, that influence our emotions on a more cellular level (similar to animals who mark territory with scent for other animals to pick up), proving that the power of smell can actually have a major influence on how we feel in a particular environment.[1] Admittedly, I hadn't picked up on a scent in my above example, but I'd certainly "picked up" on something.

I believe our ability to sense energy goes beyond our five primary senses – and clearly beyond five centuries too.

Children seem to be more receptive to tuning in to the frequencies around them, but that's not to say there are not ways we can develop our ability as adults to sense the energy that exists around us, and come up with ways to influence the energy we give off so that our grooming environment (or any other environment for the matter) will have a better chance of giving off the right signals to our animals and their guardians.

Our own feelings and emotions leave a mark on our environment and influence those around us also.

Have you ever walked into a room and noticed a piercing intensity? Or perhaps visited a church and felt completely peaceful?

The ambience in a room can be influenced by many things – light, temperature, sound, texture (all of which we will get into more in chapters to come), but the one we often forget to consider is *ourselves*. Our emotions are key, and they are even more powerful than we could ever imagine.

ACTIVITY

Start observing how you feel when you enter a room. Notice the body language and behaviours of the people around you. Pay attention to how this is making you feel. Do you feel happy, sad, tense? Do you feel, relaxed or energised? What do you *really* feel?

It helps to take a brief moment to set your intention before entering a space, especially when you are just beginning to practice this exercise. Eventually, all of this will become a habit and you will start to notice rather quickly what places to avoid, and how to influence how you give and receive energy in different situations.

Being mindful of the energy around us is one of the many ways we can begin to influence the very atmosphere of our grooming space, making it more relaxing for our animals - and ourselves.

Developing Our Empathy and Compassion

Did you know that empathy is said to be a form of telepathy? Empathy is the skill of physically feeling the emotion of another person, animal, plant or other living organism. Empaths are extremely sensitive to emotion and can have a hard time processing the information they receive.

The mirror neuron system is a specialised group of brain cells that researchers have discovered are responsible for compassion. The cells work by mirroring emotions, allowing a person to feel another individual's pain, happiness or suffering[9]. Empaths are more receptive to intense physical feeling, which can have a detrimental impact on their own psychological, emotional and physical health. A blessing and a curse, perhaps.

But developing our empathy and compassion is fundamental in working with animals, because it allows us to put ourselves in their pawprints. When we are compassionate, we have the ability to come from the canine perspective and see the grooming environment through the eyes of our dogs, and that, my friends, changes everything!

One of the ways many spiritual practices like to expand on their compassion and empathy is through the activation of their third eye chakra – all of which are interlinked.

Developing Our Subliminal Connection

Some people believe that dogs have a 'sixth sense'.

Yet in humans, the concept of being 'psychic' is still generally quite a controversial topic, and it is true that many scientists still disregard the idea based on little evidence to support it.

Spiritualists believe that all living animals are made up of chakras, and in humans, the third eye chakra brings balance between our logical brain and our creative one. It's said that bringing the two sides of our brain together activates our intuition, enabling us to see things that aren't physically there.[10] Fascinating, isn't it!

Yes Steph, but how is this relevant to Holistic Grooming exactly?

Well, animals have been known to pick up on vibrations in the environment to sense weather changes - such as earthquakes and tsunamis - moments before they occur. It could be said these are animals with a higher sense of intuition than us, no?

We also know that some dogs can be easily trained as service dogs, owing to their ability to pick up on seizures and fits before they even happen in their guardians.

My point is, if dogs can do it (and their brains are not near as advanced as ours), then why can't we? And if we *could* learn to harness such skills, couldn't we use this to help us enhance our communication and relationships with dogs in the grooming environment even more?

Imagine that for a moment: a groomer who could use the power of energy to send out a message to instil calm in an environment, enough to influence anyone and anything who enters the room to feel that same calm.

True Story

I was walking one of my dogs, King Louis (great name, I know!) through the park one evening and decided to take the route we call "the back hills", which really is just a series of dirt tracks that takes you alongside a river, surrounded by hills.

As we walked down the path, I noticed a shift in Louis' energy. Every step was slow and deliberate and he was alert to all sounds around us. I could tell he wasn't entirely sure of what it was he was feeling at this point exactly, despite having made this trip many times.

Reassuring him as we continued down the dirt path, we came across a van in the distance that was parked in the middle of another path ahead – blocking our exit, essentially. A man emerged from behind the vehicle, dressed all in black and slowly pacing around as though he was waiting on someone.

It was odd considering this wasn't a place of parking and I must admit I felt a little intimidated about trying to move around the obstruction as I approached it. But I didn't need to worry, because Louis stopped dead in his tracks, staring down the man in the distance. He puffed out his mane and stood squarely. Hackles were up, ears were alert and I knew he wasn't happy.

He didn't make a sound as the man stopped his pacing and looked straight at us.

At that moment, Louis yanked me back in the direction we had come from. There's no fighting against a 90kg Tibetan Mastiff, so I let him lead the way to safety.

Although I suspected that the man was potentially quite strange, Louis knew something I didn't. Clearly, the man wasn't to be trusted, and I genuinely believe I could have been in danger if it wasn't for Louis' intuition. I still get goosebumps telling that story and I've never walked that route again since.

When you look at what science has now discovered when it comes to mirroring emotions, I believe it's only a matter of time before it reveals that in fact, it is more than possible for us to activate both the logical, and creative side of our brains simultaneously to broaden our connection with all living things around us.

7

IT STARTS WITH 'SELF'

"Sitting on your feelings isn't a good idea. They just get squashed that way."

— RICHARD TEMPLAR

ARGUABLY, THIS CHAPTER SHOULD HAVE BEEN THE OPENING OF this book because everything starts with me, you, US. How we look after ourselves, how we express our feelings, how we understand what we need and distinguish it from what we *want*.

But why are self-care and self-love so important?

Because (*echo alert*): everything is connected to everything else! We are all connected, we are all energy beings responding to one another constantly.

What's more, when we work in an industry that involves caring for others, AND using sharp objects on fully-conscious animals, we must (and I mean, MUST) be sure that we are of sound mind. We are healthy, we are calm and we are confident.

Just as we'll be regularly servicing our scissors, and clippers, we must also ensure that we're taking good care of *ourselves*.

I repeat, your health and wellbeing are just as important as the dogs – you cannot expect one without the other.

Let's start with the basics first…

What you NEED vs what you WANT

I *want* to eat a tub of Ben and Jerry's every night after dinner, but my body sure as hell doesn't *need* the extra calories, so I need to think about what's best for my health, right?

In order for our bodies to thrive as the living organisms they are, we need to ensure that we are looking after it properly, and that means also looking at ourselves from a - you guessed it - holistic point of view.

ACTIVITY

Ask yourself the following questions:

What makes me feel healthy?

What makes me feel strong?

What makes me feel energised?

What makes me feel happy?

For Example:

Is Holistic Grooming for you, or do you want to compete in Professional Styling?

I am in awe of some of our industry's most dedicated stylists, who spend hours and hours... and hours of their time practicing scissor work, learning what all the different tools do (I *still* don't know the difference between thinners and blenders), and fine-tuning their attention to every angulated, symmetrical detail – boy, that's skill for you!

But all that stress and pressure to create such beautiful work comes at a price (at least initially), and it takes a bloody strong person to survive under the pressure of such a cut-throat industry that is professional styling.

Ok, so pressure can be good a good thing, and we've already established that stress is necessary to keep our autonomic nervous systems working, but for some people, the stress of having hundreds of eyes on you all the time- all while your peers are desperately hoping you will make a mistake just so that they can claim the title- is simply too much stress (for me).

For one thing, I'm certainly not brave enough to have *my* work under microscopic view, so I can tell you right off the bat that I'm not cut out for show or competition grooming – I don't need that, and true, I don't necessarily want it either.

But the thought that I'm improving an animal's health and wellbeing through what I do??? I *need* that to feel like I'm making a positive difference – that's my motivation right there!

So, with that in mind, you need to find out what makes you most passionate, and establish how you're going to do it with your needs in mind, always.

The Power of Negative Thinking

Neuroscience has proven that our brain processes a negative remark or experience faster than a positive one, and that if we are distracted from a good event before the positive experience is logged in our long-term memory, it will not be stored at all (otherwise known as 'Negative Bias'). Ain't that just peachy?![1]

What's more, many a scientific study reveals the consequences that negative thinking has on our health - and on our physical performance too!

So, let's concentrate more on happy thoughts (think Peter Pan).

The Good/Bad Apple Experiment

Inspired by Dr. Masaru Emoto's wonderful theory about water[2], Danielle La Porte decided to conduct her own experiment into positive and negative thinking...

Two halves of the same apple were placed in their own sealed jar on a windowsill.

Throughout each day (over approximately 25),

members of the La Porte family would speak to each of the jars.

One was the "Apple of Positivity". The other was the "Apple of Negativity".

The Positivity Apple would receive compliments and happy vibes, whilst the Negativity Apple would receive insults and angry vibes.

After approximately 25 days, the apple of positivity had managed to stay preserved, whilst the apple of negativity was rotten.[3]

Try And Stay Mindful

Of course, we're talking about dogs rather than apples here, but if an apple can suffer under the weight of negative thinking, then where that emotionally leaves a living, sentient being is worthy of exploring too, no?

When we anticipate how a grooming session is going to go, we are *influencing* how the grooming session will go, so don't underestimate the power of your thought!

It is more likely for a dog to misbehave or be aggressive when we anticipate that the dog will misbehave in the first place. I'm told that this is exactly the same for children…

And so, we can become more aware of the danger in stereotyping, so that we can be more positive in our approach to all animals as individuals instead. Simple!

We Suppress Emotions Too

As we delve into this topic, you will probably begin to notice the incredible similarities between us and dogs, which is no accident. The very concept of Holistic Grooming is to emphasise the relevance of just how intimate the bond that we share with them is.

Unlike dogs, humans have learned how to suppress emotion[4], resulting in many negative behaviours like frustration, anger, and indeed, one of our most common health conditions in the modern world, stress. Whether it is down to our culture, or our individual fears of showing vulnerability to our peers, hiding how we really feel really is a world-wide crisis.

In fact, according to research conducted at Harvard Medical School, chronic stress is a result of unresolved emotions that trigger your autonomic nervous system (more specifically, your sympathetic nervous system's fight or flight response).[5] Just like dogs, the activation of the SNS results in many additional chronic, and recurring health conditions including:

- Bloating, nausea and sickness
- Neck, head and jaw pain/tension
- Tension headaches and migraines

It's important for us to understand that emotions make us who we are, and they also help to develop our compassion towards others, and just like any other living organism we rely on allowing energy to flow freely (without judgement and/or expectation) to prevent our own prolonged suffering too.

We Must Nurture Ourselves

Isn't it sad that very little job descriptions ever include the act of self-care? Especially considering mental health disorders are no longer a 'taboo' subject – perhaps, like commercial grooming, they simply need time to evolve?

Self-care (and self-love) is very much relevant to our productivity, I believe, because if we aren't feeling good, then our enthusiasm diminishes. When we have no passion, our love of the job is no longer there, and when we no longer love our jobs – you get it, it's a domino effect!

We need to feel good, to do good.

So why wouldn't we spend time self-reflecting, and researching ways to ensure we stay healthy?

I'm not just talking about:

1. What we eat and drink.
2. How often we exercise, and
3. Our quality of sleep.

But, also:

4. Connecting to our intuition (our "third eye").
5. Connecting to nature (and embracing the healing of nature), and
6. Embracing our individuality.

EXAMPLE:

You play the violin in a 30-piece orchestra, made up of some of the world's greatest musicians. Together, you all make the most beautiful music wherever you go. But during a performance one evening, a string from your violin snaps, knocking the entire production off balance.

Your violin has been overplayed and overworked, which has put a strain not only on you, but also on the rest of the musicians (and the performance).

The only way you can resolve the problem is to repair the broken string - or find yourself a new violin. Hopefully not a new orchestra.

The human body is like an orchestra, in this case. When one thing is broken and/or out of tune, then our entire body is in a weakened and often vulnerable state. It puts on a poor performance.

- We lack concentration
- We make mistakes
- We become overly emotional
- We struggle to retain information or remember things
- We become more irritable and we anger easily
- We are tense and find it difficult to get to sleep

And the list goes on.

Alas, we are stuck with the bodies we have and it's not as easy as buying another, like we might consider in my example about the violin. Instead, we have to nurture ourselves and try our best to make sure that we don't overwork and abuse what we have – and what we need.

If we don't, eventually our bodies will break down, and we will begin to see signs of illness, not only that our relationships will suffer too.

1. Embracing A Healthy Diet

There's an old saying that *"you are what you eat"*, and though I'm not saying you are literally a cow because you eat beef (you may be a cow, but who am I to judge?), what I *am* saying is that the quality of the food source is what makes the real difference.

Genetically modified produce is everywhere, and even the very air in which we breathe is polluted. Therefore, is it really possible to find organic, untainted produce that is completely good for us?

Probably not.

But there are ways in which we can reduce the number of pesticides and chemicals we consume through responsible sourcing.

- We can grow our own vegetables and herbs at home
- We can reduce our consumption of fast-foods
- We can eat more fresh food (non-frozen, in other words)
- We can eat less meat and dairy
- We can implement a more plant-based diet
- We can take vitamins and supplements

2. Exercise (And Stretching!)

Keeping our bodies fit enables us to cope better with longer working hours - and physically demanding tasks, such as grooming.

There's no denying that professional grooming/styling can be strenuous on our bodies and minds. Strength-building exercises will help us to develop our muscles and improve our posture to enable us to feel strong, thus reducing the risk of injury. And, there are loads of different types of exercise you can try, so it's your job to find something that works for you, based on what you need and enjoy.

PS. If you're a busy working mama like me, who seldom has five-minutes of alone time because your children want to follow you everywhere (and I mean EVERYWHERE), then walking the dogs and stretching might be good enough for now!

According to the staff at the world-renowned Mayo Clinic[6], the benefits of daily walks include:

- Keeps the pounds off with less intensity
- Preventing heart disease and other health conditions
- Strengthens muscle and bones
- Clears your head of messy thoughts
- Works on your balance and coordination (this seems to have skipped me, I'll be honest)

And, according to Preferred Physical Therapy[7], the benefits of stretching alone include:

- Improved flexibility and posture
- Prevention of loss of motion in the joints
- Decreased back pain
- Prevention of injury
- Reduction in soreness and stiffness

Plus, I've found that stretching really gives me an instant energy release and boost (and who doesn't need one of those on the hour, right?)

So, yay for stretching!

3. <u>Getting Enough Sleep</u>

One of the most common causes of ill-health and depression is sleep deprivation – and as a species we seem to be terrible at switching-off.

But why?

Some reasons include:

- Stress
- Demanding working hours
- Using electronic devices too close to bedtime
- Using social media to switch off (newsflash - it does exactly the opposite)
- A noisy, hot and/or uncomfortable sleeping environment
- Medical problems including depression, chronic pain and insomnia

It's important for us to get at least 7.5-8 hours of sleep per day (night) in order to properly function and to perform tasks to the best of our ability. However, lack of sleep can cause a chain reaction of health conditions and symptoms that can take their toll on our physical and mental capabilities.[8]

More specifically, as dog groomers and stylists, some of the risks of sleep deprivation can prove to be more dangerous than others, due to our requirement to concentrate and to operate sharp, potentially life-threatening equipment. We suffer a reduced attention span, slow reaction rates, and lack of concentration. It's not great!

Getting into a routine each night to help encourage a good night's rest is therefore crucial.

We can do this in numerous ways, including:

- Going for a relaxing stroll (perhaps with your dog)
- Taking a warm bath/shower with lavender scents or oils
- Investing in black-out curtains, ear plugs and a sleep mask
- Refreshing your bed covers and pyjamas regularly
- Switching off electronic devices an hour before bedtime
- Reading a good book in bed
- Sipping a chamomile tea or hot chocolate
- Investing in a journal and brain dumping!

And, one of the best ways I have found to get a peaceful night's sleep is through Holistic Grooming itself. Go on, give your dog a cuddle and comb!

4. <u>Connecting to ourselves</u>

What does it mean to really connect with ourselves?

With the introduction of social media and instant messaging platforms, the opportunity to be bored and/or spend quiet time alone with our thoughts and feelings is limited at best.

As we already know, it's too easy to suppress emotions, because nobody wants to show that they are unhappy, unsatisfied or vulnerable. We look at what others are doing and immerse ourselves in their lives, allowing incurable cases of 'comparisonitus' (yes, I've just made that word up) to set in.

The point is: it's not healthy, whatever side you're on.

Learn to be ok with feeling vulnerable, for the sake of your own self-development if nothing else (remember good ole' Brené Brown!).

When we bottle up our feelings, it eats away at our self-worth and we begin to self-loathe - and self-sabotage our lives.

The fear of getting to the cause of *why* we feel a certain way stops us from overcoming destructive habits.

But there's only so long we can put a face on before we finally have to face the music, and putting off the inevitable is a fast-track ticket to misery (I know, because I've been there!).

The fact is, we are emotional, living beings, and experiencing the highs and lows is completely normal – expect them, embrace them... then let them pass!

"Let it pass."

— STEPHANIE ZIKMANN

Note: counselling sessions are a great investment to your self-care regime (or calling on Mental Health Helplines), and can be a healthy way to express your emotions in a healthy way, without feeling like you are weighing down on your loved ones.

Stay Authentic

I want to also encourage you to be authentic and true to yourself because I genuinely believe this is very important in safeguarding your happiness.

True Story

Over the last two years I have been at the firing end of trolling on social media merely because I genuinely don't agree with the status quo that makes up commercial grooming. My views on the grooming industry have caused a ripple, to say the least, that led to some challenging times for me both personally and professionally.

Amongst some of the abusive comments I received, I saw statements like, "you're not a real groomer", and "you're not experienced enough to be educating anyone", "you're a nobody", and "you're a snowflake".

At first, I was devastated (and angry). Then sadly, I started to wonder if those statements were indeed true, as the doubt under the weight of the comments set in. None of those feelings were pleasant.

Imposter syndrome is a killer of dreams – remember that.

There was a moment when I thought about giving up, but then I remembered why I was doing what I do. Ambition takes guts, and it's important to remember that you cannot possibly please everyone.

I now try to show compassion to everyone, especially the trolls who called me names, because I now know these are the very kinds of people who most need my understanding – and the information this book can give them!

ACTIVITY

Digital Detox Time!

1. **The next time someone bad-mouths you, or trolls you on social media – forgive them, then let it go. Respect that without difference of opinions, we wouldn't be beautifully individual and authentic – it takes many colours to make a rainbow, right?!**
2. **It's far better to accept there will be people who aren't on your wavelength, than to try tirelessly to convince them to believe in what you do. Don't get preachy – talk to those who want to listen.**
3. **Surround yourself with those who love, and respect**

you. It's time to virtually (or physically) remove the people who don't from your circle of influence. A Digital Detox can do wonders to your mental health, so go through your friends list now (yes, NOW!) and delete the haters.

Note: Don't aspire to surround yourself with "yes" men either – you need people around you who can be honest and tell you when you've made a mistake. The difference is that they support you in a way that helps you grow.

Let me know how you feel!

Channel Your Fear Of Being Vulnerable

Many of us allow fear to get in the way of our education, our progress and our success – the fear of being wrong, the fear of being right, the fear of being judged, the fear of being judged (oh yeah, said that already), the fear of being laughed at, the fear of being questioned yourself.

The truth is, we are all afraid, and we feel all the more vulnerable when we are doing something that is important to us. It's normal that we would want to do anything to avoid feeling the shame of being wrong - or dare I say being thought of as 'stupid'.

That's an emotional default of humans – not sure if that's a fact, I admit, but I certainly believe so. But there's hope for us all, and it comes down to mindset.

"Shame resilience is the ability to practice authenticity when we experience shame, to move through the experience without sacrificing our values, and to come out on the other side of the shame experience with more courage, compassion and connection than we had going into it.[9]"

— BRENÉ BROWN, *DARE TO LEAD*

'Shame' Researcher Brené believes that when we allow ourselves to embrace and then let go of our fears, we become more open to receiving the opinions of others. And it makes total sense based on what we now know about energy and emotions, right?

Feelings are meant to keep flowing in order for us to develop.

Could fear be the reason why our industry (and many others) is still trying to play catch-up with modern science?

Fear can be valuable when it's utilised into courage.

Courage isn't the absence of fear. Therefore, it's time to be brave my friends – part of Holistic Grooming is about staying loyal to our ethical approach, no matter the influence in front of us. Be brave. Stay true. Be *You*.

Avoiding Burnout

In Chapter 8: Part Two we will talk about a dog called Max who bit his owner after a stressful trip to the salon. A prime example of burnout in a dog due to trigger stacking.

It could be YOU next!

Have you bitten anyone recently?

I hope the answer was no, but stranger things…

Whilst we may not express emotional overload the way that Max did, if we aren't careful, humans can express burnout in undesirable ways, too.

The trick is (and we all like a good trick as much as the next dog), is to develop our intuition and reconnect with our emotions *as we are feeling them.*

One of the ways I do this is through colour prompts in my working/at-home environments, through something called *The Colour Dot Exercise For Busy Minds*:

ACTIVITY

Before I start my day, I stick a range of coloured dotted stickers on different places and surfaces in my salon.

Every single time I see a dot, I ask myself:

What do I *need?*

How does my environment *feel?*

Are the dogs in the salon being affected by my energy?

What is the *cause* of this feeling?

How do I change my underlying emotional state?

Quick tip if you try this - change where you put the dots every day so that you don't get used to the positioning of them and therefore no longer notice them.

There are other patterns and routines you can try. Have a quick google, then pick one that appeals to/ works for you.

Failing to check in with ourselves when we are at work is one of the leading reasons why we wake up one day to find ourselves out-of-love with our job with seemingly little way back. I want Holistic Grooming to be something you can fall more and more in love with each day – not something you're dreading to wake up to.

Back To Balance

We need to find a way to bring ourselves back to balance – it really is that simple.

Just like with dogs, we need to avoid filling our cup and going over our own threshold. We need to know our limits. When you're one dog fart away from a mini-meltdown, you are well and truly in need of some deep-breathing and meditation my friends! Never (ever) underestimate the power of journaling and recording your experiences, also.

Meditation and Deep Breathing

Deep breathing and meditation are common practice amongst most holistic therapies for humans, but I love using Holistic Grooming to utilise my daily mindfulness practice in a way that benefits both myself and the animal at the same time.

In Let Animals Lead™ Reiki for example, meditation is a big part of the 'intent to heal' process and is a fantastic way to connect and enhance our bond with the animal in front of us (remember to seek Guardian and Vet permission, and obtain at least, your Level 2).

The key with meditation is to start slowly because some people find it extremely hard to "switch off". But when we set ourselves smaller, more achievable tasks we instantly increase

With that in mind, the easiest way to implement meditation into our working lives is to first develop the habit of slowing down for a few minutes several times throughout the working day.

ACTIVITY

Note down today's date:

```
┌─────────────────────────────┐
│                             │
│                             │
│                             │
└─────────────────────────────┘
```

Over the next 4 weeks, I want you to make a point of meditating for at least five minutes - twice a day.

Let's make it even easier... every time you go to the toilet, I want you to meditate. And, if you don't have enough time to go to the toilet in a day... see a doctor!

During each meditation, ask yourself how you are feeling. Just sit (possibly on the toilet) with those feelings for a few moments, before coming back down to Earth.

At the end of the 4 weeks, note down how you feel below:

Has your general health improved?

- **Yes**
- **No**

The purpose of this activity is to start developing a habit of listening to your body and listening to what it is telling you.

5. Connecting With Nature

"It is in the wisdom and sacred teachings of Indigenous people across the world...they have the deepest connection to the spirit of the Earth and its history, and from this intimacy, healing can occur."[10]

— JAMES MASKALYK & DAVE COURCHENE.

I love that statement.

There are numerous studies around the benefits of being in nature when it comes to health and wellness, with scientists calling it "ecopsychology".

According to scientists, it takes only 120 minutes to begin to feel the long-term benefits of nature, based on a study of 20,000 people split across two groups. After spending two hours a week in nature spots, all participants reported feeling happier and healthier at the end of each week. Those who never reached the two-hour threshold reported no differences to their mood.[11]

We can spend more time in nature in many ways:

- Forest bathing - alone or with our dogs
- Camping and hiking
- Tree hugging (perhaps it isn't so crazy after-all)
- Reiki in nature
- Litter picking

Science has also shown that the benefits of immersing yourself in nature include:

- Lowered blood pressure
- Reduced production of stress hormones
- Reduction of stress responses (sympathetic nervous system activation)
- Reduced anxiety
- Increased self-esteem

- Improved overall mood
- Decreased ADHD symptoms
- Decreased aggression

We can make the most of our time in nature by allowing our pets to join us for those joyful moments of rest.

ACTIVITY

Set aside <u>two-hours</u> a week to spend time in nature (remember it MUST be two-hours).

Insert Date Here:

Insert Date Four Weeks From the Start Date:

What Have You Noticed in this Time?

Self-Worth

The only one who gets to decide your worth is you. It doesn't come from your bank account, or the number of friends you have. It doesn't come from what someone else says you are worth.

It's called self-love for a reason – it comes from you. It comes from being yourself and being proud of who you are.

It comes from being someone that you can count on, and someone you love. The numbers will change with time, but what won't change is who you are deep inside – beautiful, limitless, wonderful, creative, strong, capable – and that is where your worth comes from.

— Nikki Banas, 'Shine From Within'.

8

THE HOLISTIC GROOMING PROTOCOL

"Knowledge of constitution is the key for a holistic and integral health care, the true basis of any preventative medicine."

— VASANT LAD

IN CHAPTER ONE WE BROKE DOWN ELEMENTS TO CONSIDER when coming from the Canine Perspective, but I want to now go back into it in more detail because it's important that we encourage your brain to get into the habit of thinking this way.

I devised the Holistic Grooming Protocol as a way to help me remember to think outside the box with some of my most challenging dogs, but it has actually helped me with every single one (including my own dogs at home!).

Part One – The Grooming Environment

It all begins with 'N.O.T.T.S.S' (hopefully not actual *knots*), but rather the environmental stressors we can manage, and how we can consider the senses in our planning, and approach.

As follows:

Noise – what can the dog hear? Music? Traffic? Alarms? Shop Shutters? Window Cleaners? Postmen? Deliveries? Sirens? One of the main triggers of stress for dogs are actually those that are noise-related, due to the animal's acute sense of hearing.

Objects – what can the dog see? Roller banners? People passing? Reflections? Other animals? Remember things look a whole lot scarier when you're small.

Texture – what can the dog feel? Vinyl flooring? Safety flooring? Rubber? A rug? Carpet? Is it slippery? Is it rough? Is it comfortable?

Taste – what can the dog taste? Cleaning products from dog bowls and other surfaces? What about treats available? Are you using LickiMats and Snuffle Mats? If so, do you need paste? What about allergies – both guardians and dogs?

Smell – what can the dog smell? Other dogs? Bitches in season? Cleaning products? Air freshener? Is it too strong? Is it too clinical? Are you using essential oils? Candles? Pet Remedy?

Spirituality – how does the environment feel? How do I feel? What vibrations am I sending into the atmosphere? How does the energy feel? Am I sending the right message?

As I've said, the grooming environment can always be adapted to help relax and decrease the anxiety of an animal in our care. It's our job to think creatively and come up with ways to do so.

Conducting the Phone Consultation

The very first thing that all groomers should do, is call a prospective guardian to discuss things over the phone. In The Holistic Grooming Diploma, students learn how to implement careful planning to ensure they are backed with the right information to set the very first impressions up for success. Needless to say, this is the most crucial part of the Holistic Grooming Protocol™.

Guardians should note that it is important to spend the time in discussing their dog's history, lifestyle and requirements with honesty and transparency. A lot of the planning relies on the information given by the guardian.

Preparing the Environment for a Meet and Treat

The Meet and Treat service is the foundation a Holistic Groomer will set that will be significant to the dog upon first arrival at the salon.

While it's easy for a guardian to set up a home environment to suit the needs of their pet, it gets slightly more difficult to adapt the environment of a commercial salon to suit every individual dog. But that doesn't mean it isn't possible to make it, at the very least, less stressful.

Remember: environmental stressors are EVERYWHERE.

Even more so in environments where noise is unavoidable, amongst other nasties that animals with heightened senses may not appreciate (clangs of metal, the scent of other nervous animals etc.).

Boy, it really is hard being a dog!

But before you start ripping out your hair with frustration, just stop, BREATHE, and think about things logically based on the information you have in front of you.

Think: holistic – means as a whole. What is the WHOLE environment telling you?

PS. You've got this!

With a little creative flair and thinking-outside-the-box, there are numerous ways we can reduce the intensity of the stressors in our working environment. It's about getting into the habit of asking ourselves the right questions, then waiting for the penny to drop!

SURVEY

A survey conducted within numerous Veterinary practices in the UK set out to investigate the current measures in place to prevent stress in the animal care environment, and to pinpoint the areas needing re-evaluation for maximum calmness in their animal patients.

The results concluded that whilst the majority of practices use treats before, during and after an appointment to help build positive experiences, and that their handling was good in the process, there were areas that could be improved, such as providing separate waiting areas for different pets and playing classical music in those areas as they waited.[1]

There will always (always!) be room for improvement, and the more we develop our understanding as the years progress, the more the demand for adapting our approach will be.

And just when you think you've finally got a handle on everything, it is time to get on your knees and look at it from the canine's perspective – and I mean each dog's individual perspective too!

Yes, I'm being literal again. And No, I'm not joking. It genuinely works.

An Additional Note On Energy In The Environment

It's important for the Holistic Groomer (in fact, EVERYONE!) to be mindful of negative thinking, especially when it comes to the anticipation of how a session is going to go.

I'm talking about the groomer who believes that every Chow Chow is aggressive, or that every Westie wants to claw your eyes out (remember the harm in stereotyping?).

Just remember that a negative mindset makes for a negative experience. And who wants that?!

"We project our fears into the world, so our animal and human friends act them out. When this happens, you might think you had a premonition that something bad was going to happen, but in actuality, the thought you sent was received by that dog and encouraged him to do exactly what you did not want."

— AMELIA KINKADE, THE LANGUAGE OF MIRACLES

When we refer back to the flaws in some of our most outdated legislation and laws, we know that it can be hard to step away from the habit of labelling, especially when we have been brainwashed into believing it since the very beginning.

Old habits *are* hard to break, but as the saying goes: "an old dog CAN learn new tricks", and of course, you can too!

EXERCISE

Repeat after me:

I promise to try my best to look at each dog as an individual, sentient being with no labels, no stereotypes, and no expectations so that they are given the best chance of being their best selves from the beginning.

Recap: Why Dogs Find Grooming Stressful

Since the duties of the Holistic Groomer involves styling, we must consider the reasons why dogs generally seem to find the commercial grooming environment as stressful as they do.

We now know that a dog's heritage, genetics, past experiences, and environment can influence fear, but have we ever considered:

1. The difficulty of the process itself? The introduction of mix-breeds with difficult coat types makes grooming a more strenuous process for some dogs, where gentle strokes and the occasional snip here and there just ain't going to cut it! Literally.

2. Guardian expectations? Some guardians are so convinced that the role of the groomer is easy, even fun, that they expect instant results under strict timeframes. This is dangerous in itself and proves to be a leading cause of stress in all grooming establishments.

3. The grooming routine outside the salon? Guardians seldom realise the responsibility they have in keeping up with grooming at home irrespective of coat demands (but especially with high-maintenance coats). Having the dog groomed daily, in a positive way will help to keep them resilient and confident too. If your guardians aren't aware, then it's time to show them.

Part Two – The Canine Perspective

"A healthy outside starts with a healthy inside."

— ROBERT URICH

Then we think about our most important tool - OURSELVES. Considering:

- **Speaking 'Dog'** - What is our behaviour, body language, approach and handling saying to the dog? Are we confident or are we apprehensive? Are we calm or are we anxious?
- **Our Positioning** – can we sit side on and sit low (perhaps on a foot stool)? Avoid leaning over a dog or reaching out our hand for anything. Don't force or initiate interaction. Avoid petting the top of the head - and remember that the back of our hand is better than our palm. Avoid direct and sustained eye-contact, and remember to keep our energy calm and positive.
- **Our Behaviour** - adapt dog behaviours/body language into our own. Don't over-smile (in dog language showing teeth is a warning signal). We can yawn and avert our gaze to show we are not a threat and we can even initiate play with a play bow when it's safe (I do this a lot with puppies).
- **Our Training Technique** - stock up on a range of treats (confirm allergies with the guardian prior to this). Food is a good way to establish trust and build a positive experience. Implementing snuffle mats and/or LickiMats into the environment is a good way to engage the dog's mind and to build up a positive association with the environment at the same time.
- **Our Overall Approach** – non-grooming appointments can be arranged to gradually work at

introducing the dog to the environment through desensitisation, classical or operant conditioning and positive reinforcement. Use this time to introduce the environment and grooming/styling process at a comfortable pace for the dog.

- **Our Problem-Solving Skills** – what about breaking the groom up into achievable chunks with either a few mini breaks between each significant part (break between the bath and dry, break between the dry and style etc), or a bath and dry one day and a clip on another?

- **Our Other Resources** - considering having the guardian wash and dry their dog the night before, to enable us to style only the following day. Or asking that the guardian stays with us to help handle and observe the dog during the groom. This is a great time to educate the guardian - and show them our value at the same time.

- **Our State of Mind** – being kind to ourselves and the dog. We must stop aiming for perfection, rather aim for easy-maintenance. Unrealistic expectations are soul destroying, and it won't take long before we start resenting our job. Be compassionate.

When To Schedule An Appointment

The handler should always consider the few days on the lead up to an appointment, the hours before the appointment itself, and the next few days after the appointment to reduce the likelihood of the dog being too stressed for a groom.

The reason we want to avoid bringing a dog who is already aroused into the grooming environment is that we are less likely to have a successful training experience.

Avoiding the likes of:

- Vet Trips
- Kennel Trips
- Bitches on Heat
- Lactating Bitches
- During A House Flit
- Shortly After A Family Bereavement
- And other significant incidents that result in the dog being overly aroused

Remembering that dogs are highly emotional and sentient beings that require *at least* a few days to allow themselves to return to a Parasympathetic State (though this varies a great deal with each dog), where they will be naturally more responsive to learning experiences.

The Right Training Methods

Remember I mentioned before that groomers kinda *are,* or *should* be trainers (and behaviourists)? That's because many of our dogs will need time to adapt to the grooming environment, but the process can progress much faster if we learn how to work with dogs in a more positive and efficient way. Dogs love to be mentally stimulated – if we catch their attention *before* the Autonomic Nervous System is engaged, then we can help them better through learning.

But before we do, we need to understand what training methods are acceptable.

Desensitisation with Positive Reinforcement - The purpose of this approach is to gradually introduce each external stimulus to the dog at his own pace, to enable him to adjust to the environment in a positive way.

Rather than confuse you with the quadrants of Operant Conditioning (and myself for the matter), let's stick to what we need to know in order to carry out our roles in Holistic Grooming positively and safely.

Mini Glossary

Positive Reinforcement - adding something positive the dog will like/enjoy to encourage a desired behaviour.

The Holistic Grooming environment should remain positive at all times, and the groomer should avoid any form of negative, corrective, or punishing techniques. This includes the use of aversive tools, unreasonable force, corrector sprays, and even raising our voices.

We can choose a reward based on the dog's specific likes and interests – some are motivated by food, while others are motivated by play, scent-work, praise, petting etc.

When a dog appears to be unmotivated by all potential rewards, we must evaluate the situation and assess whether he is perhaps too far over his threshold.

Counter-Conditioning (CC) and Desensitisation (DS) with Positive Reinforcement (PR) - When a dog displays a more severe fear response to a particular stimulus, the Holistic Groomer will choose this approach. The purpose of CC/DS is to change the underlying emotional state that the dog has already learned through a past experience.

It's important that the groomer does all they can to get to the cause of the fear, so that they can try to resolve the very source of the behaviour, and avoid suppressing an underlying emotion. Therefore, we can utilise all we have learnt in this book thus far to determine what we are trying to counter-condition a response to.

This approach takes time, and careful observation to prevent the dog exceeding his emotional load. The reward is simultaneous with the fear stimulus, even when the undesired behaviour is being displayed This is to change the dogs emotional state from negative to positive.

**Operant Conditioning and Positive Reinforcement - ** This is the technique a groomer might use to encourage the dog to do something else, instead of an undesired behaviour. A reward is given to the dog immediately *after*, and then sometimes simultaneously while he performs the alternative, desired behaviour in the presence of the trigger.

EXAMPLE:

1. You have a dog who will lunge towards the hair dryer whenever you switch it on.

2. To change his association, you decide to train the dog with a "look at me" command, using a high-level reward (in this case hot dogs). You get the dog's attention before activating the stimulus, and then gradually introduce it using desensitisation (at a distance that doesn't activate a negative response). The dog is then rewarded simultaneously with the noise of the hair dryer in the distance.

3. The important thing to remember is that the alternative action must be enjoyable for the dog in order to successfully change the dog's association with the dryer from negative to positive.

4. After a few short, and positive sessions, you will be able to successfully switch the hair dryer on without the dog lunging. Instead, he will look at you, having learned that something positive and enjoyable happens when the hair dryer comes out.

Suppressed Emotions in The Grooming Environment

There are typically two ways we can cause suppressed emotions in the grooming environment.

1. We may try to control the behaviour through the use of

aversive tools and/or methods that are outdated and ineffective long term.

2. We may try to manage the behaviour through the use of operant conditioning, using positive methods.

Whatever the case may be, when we aren't looking at the *cause* of the behaviour itself, we are encouraging the dog to suppress his emotions, rather than let the energy flow.

Remember: emotion means "energy in motion", so what's inside, must come out.

Let's look at an example...

Case Study

Max is a 12-year-old German Shepherd Dog with elbow dysplasia. He visits the groomers for a haircut once a year and usually copes well.

Today however, Max is clearly not happy. He is pulled into the bath against his will and begins to struggle against the groomer. He is panting excessively, his tail is tucked, and his ears are pinned back.

The groomer asks the guardian to leave because that could be distracting Max.

Due to his resistance, the groomer decides to secure Max on the grooming table with the 'Groomer's Helper' – a device that prevents a dog jumping, turning or sitting down. Though the groomer likely doesn't intend this, she has now removed Max's option to rest if needed, and also his ability to flee if it all gets too much.

As the groomer dries him using a High Velocity dryer, Max's emotions escalate and his autonomic nervous system activates his sympathetic nervous system into fight mode (remember, he can't flee). He begins to air snap, pull, and snarl at the groomer, who then decides an additional restraint is required. She opts for a muzzle and cone to further protect herself from being bitten.

Max continues to fight until he tires himself out. He stops fighting and appears to be standing contently. The groomer is pleased and believes that she has successfully desensitised him to the process.

The reality is that Max has actually gone into 'shut down' mode – the result of trigger stacking and subsequently emotional overload/the suppression of emotions.

Two hours have passed, and Max is finally off the table and feeling exhausted. It will take time and rest for the adrenalin in his system to come back into balance.

Back home his guardian is unaware of how Max is feeling and decides to wake him from his sleep in an attempt to put his harness on to go his evening walk.

Max awakes abruptly and bites his guardian on the hand.

Summary:

Not allowing an animal to naturally express their emotions in the grooming environment (or any environment) can result in the escalation of undesired behaviours. Failing to recognise that Max was either afraid or in pain resulted in the suppression of his emotions, causing him to release pent-up energy in an explosive way in both the short and the long term. This is actually a very common thing to occur post-groom!

What's more, Max could have easily bitten the groomer, another dog within the grooming environment, or even a child which would most likely result in his destruction under the Dangerous Dog Act 1991 (amended 2014)!

Learning how to pick up on the early signs of fear and/or pain will enable both the guardian and the groomer to think of ways to help relieve an animal of the cause of his turmoil. Not only that, it really can save a life.

Preventing Suppressed Emotions in Dogs – The Grooming Environment

In Commercial Grooming, many of us unintentionally disrupt the energy flow in our animals through the use of restraining/handling aids, thus causing a blockage and build-up of emotions that often result in an abrupt action/behaviour, as explained previously. This is why I often say to people that the misuse of handling aids can cause our animals psychological and emotional harm without us even realising it (and don't worry, we've all done it)!

Let's face it, the more afraid a dog is, the more likely he is to try and jump, scratch, roll around to get loose increasing the risk of a physical injury to either himself or us.

ACTIVITY

Next time you think about using excessive handling restraints, put yourself in the dog's paws.

But remember, a dog has the same mental and emotional capacity as a 2-3-year-old child.

Imagine being tied to a table when you are afraid, and when you try to defend yourself, somebody adds another restraint, and another, and another.

This, my friends, is what we call: FLOODING. And I bet you would do anything to try and remove yourself from that situation (I know I would), so why are we often so surprised, or even angry that a dog responds in such a way?

Just as throwing an arachnophobe into a bath of spiders isn't going to make that person love spiders, adding more and more restraints to a dog in fear or pain is not going to help make him feel better either.

Canine perspective is a wonderful insight. Yes I am repeating myself a lot, but only because it's important.

ADAPTING **Our Approach Using Choice**

Remember we spoke in a previous chapter about Consent Grooming?

Here's a few ways the groomer could have introduced a little more choice into the scenario with Max to help him feel safer in the environment and prevent him from biting:

- She could have asked Max's guardian to stay and help. Especially with geriatric dogs, the risk of seizure is high due to stress, and the guardian being present may have helped settle him more.
- She could have let Max walk to the bath himself, using rewards and praise (because yanking and pulling against the will of a dog is a negative experience and aversive).
- She could have given Max a break between the bath and drying stages, and opted to thoroughly towel-dry him as much as possible before opting for a standing dryer, which would have put less pressure on his joints (reduce pain = reduce stress).
- She could have lowered the grooming table down to floor height or opted to groom on the floor instead, to allow Max the freedom to walk away (flee) when he needed a break. She wouldn't require handling aids to stop him from falling off the table for one, and this relaxed approach would have helped him relax too.
- She could have allowed him to rest frequently, which would have reduced Max's level of pain due to his

medical condition. It's likely that as an older dog, he has a few of those!

While I'm not saying this approach would have guaranteed a different result, what I am saying is that it would at least give Max the best chance to express his emotions safely, thus change his underlying emotion from negative to positive.

In the grooming environment, it's more than possible to implement small changes to offer our dogs more choice, and to make the entire experience less stressful all round.

The Risks of Bad Observation

Here's what we *should* now know.

A highly-aroused animal can result in,

- Defecating
- Bites and/or scratches
- Physical injury to the dog
- Psychological and/or emotional trauma
- Fainting, Seizure, heatstroke and/or heart-attack
- Damage to property, equipment and/or tools - not exactly an impact on the animal, but certainly an impact on *you*, and that's important, too!

All of the above are an indication to us that we need to do things differently. It's time to get our thinking caps on and devise a plan going forward that changes the dog's emotional state. It might mean accepting that your environment will never be suitable for him (if you are multi-groomer and the dog can't cope with too much hustle) Whatever it is, we know that some-things gotta change.

The goal of the Holistic Groomer is to stop whatever we are doing *before* the dog becomes overwhelmed with stress. The last memory is the lasting memory, so it's about doing our very best to end things positively.

During every appointment, observation and clear communication is key for mutual growth and trust building. We can even adapt a little bit of calming signals into our own behaviours to communicate to the dog that we mean no harm!

We might yawn and avert our gaze to show a dog we are no threat for example. Don't think because we aren't fluffy and don't walk on all fours that we can't speak dog too (because we can, and I do every day).

Still with me? Great, let's move on to the next step…

Part Three – How To Prepare At Home

And the last thing we need to consider is *what* the guardian can manage, and how they themselves approach things too:

- **Guardian Responsibilities** – do the guardians know what's expected of them? Do they have access to the appropriate tools? Excessive matts and tangles cause unnecessary stress, which can be avoided a whole lot better when the guardian is helping at home. Additionally, a dog who is regularly groomed will be more resilient to the excessive handling required for more complex coats, making the whole experience a little more bearable.

- **Are They Asking Questions?** – it's our job to make sure guardians feel comfortable enough to ask questions. Additionally, we can put ourselves in their shoes and try to offer peace of mind by explaining the Holistic Grooming process in detail. This will help to prevent failed expectations.
- **The Bespoke Care Plan** – we can devise a bespoke care plan that the guardians can follow, giving them a step-by-step on how often, and when to brush their dogs. Providing guardians with a grooming plan and diary to update can help motivate them to get involved in Holistic Grooming.
- **The Right Grooming Kits** – we can upsell grooming kits to suit specific coat types. This means we can be sure the guardian has the relevant tools to ensure the coat and skin can be well maintained.
- **Attending A Grooming Masterclass** – we can upsell grooming masterclasses to show guardians how to safely bathe, dry and brush their dog between professional grooming appointments. We can also demonstrate to them the appropriate handling and training methods to instil confidence and trust.
- **Continual Online Support** – we can utilise social media to provide our clients with a "client only" support group where we can post daily advice, tips, and demonstrations to help them with general enquiries and common problems.

We also have a duty of care to better prepare the guardian for the care plan at home – we should be more than willing to provide them with all the help they need in feeling confident in maintaining their dog's coat between professional grooms.

But really, guardians need to commit to grooming every day – and hopefully after reading this book, you'll want to! It really is beautiful, when it's done mindfully. Trust me.

Environmental Stress At Home

I've already mentioned that it's best to recommend that the guardian postpones any significant stressful events such as a trip to the Vet and/or kennels, the same day (and even week) as a professional grooming appointment. We want to keep their trigger stacking to a bare minimum.

Additionally, if the dog is particularly afraid of car journeys, I would be asking if it's possible that the dog walks to the salon until he has been carefully desensitised to cars. Forward-planning is key.

Being a Holistic Groomer is all about thinking outside the box and looking at the entire context:

- Where does a dog spend the majority of his day at home?
- What is his lifestyle like?
- What other pet professionals are in his life?

For example: a dog who spends the entire day barking at cars, people, and other animals, is a dog that is constantly stressed/highly aroused (his SNS is engaged). This dog will be more anxious than a dog who is kept in a room away from triggers and given plenty of mental stimulation.

Everything is relevant.

We now know that the risk of emotional overload (and erratic behaviours) is all the more likely to occur with an animal who is in a constant state of stress – not only is this bad news for the groomer, but remember it will also result in numerous chronic health conditions long term.

The 'FAS' Scale For Guardians Reference

The Fear Free Protocol™ is also available for Guardians, along with the BFF Award via the ISCP – both are great resources to instil confidence and competence in animal care. I'm also excited to be writing a course specifically for guardians looking to learn techniques in Holistic Grooming.

The point is, when dog guardians learn to familiarise themselves with Canine Behaviour, and how to handle their dog safely during grooming, they will begin to reap the healing benefits of grooming (the ancient practice).

They will also be able to recognise and identify early signs of illness too, an invaluable skill that many still take for granted.

Setting Up The Home Environment

As dog guardians we should already know that in order to keep our pets healthy, happy and free from harm between grooming appointments, we must instil a grooming routine. And of

Allowing all of these dogs to have frequent breaks, allowing them to sit when they are tired, and breaking up the groom into smaller, more achievable chunks will all help to preserve health, wellbeing and welfare.

For both geriatric and rescue dogs (and dogs with serious health problems such as cancer, or disabilities like deafness and blindness) it may be more appropriate to consider working more closely with the guardian at home, having the guardian present, and liaising with the local Vet and/or a qualified behaviourist, too.

It's all the more important to avoid:

- Unnecessary stress – caused by car journeys, long-distance travel, unfamiliar environments, loud noises, excessive handling, sudden movements, etc.
- Prolonged grooming sessions – place welfare over vanity every time. By all means clip off unwanted fur, but don't necessarily carry out a full-on styling session.
- Excessive use of handling restraints.

As groomers, we can make things easier on the dog by:

- Providing a home-visitation service where the dog is most comfortable.
- Placing a gentle hand on the dog at all times.
- Using slow and intentional movements.
- Speaking in a calm and happy voice, using lots of praise and reassurance. Remember that sound carries

vibration, so just because a deaf dog can't hear, doesn't mean he can't feel your intention.

- Offering alternative therapies such as canine massage, TTouch and/or Reiki.
- Allowing the dog to lie in a comfortable position, rather than forcing him to stand.
- Asking the guardian to help assist in order to provide comfort for the dog.

Preparing a Fearful Dog for Grooming

Fear needs understanding in order to be relieved, and so as groomers, we should always evaluate the following when grooming a rescue/fearful dog:

- The dog's history – was he badly bred? Was he abused? Was he neglected? Was he trained with dominance theory? Has he suffered any form of trauma?
- The dog's lifestyle – is he left alone all day? Is he part of a busy household? Has he got access to a safe space? Are there children in the home? Is he mentally stimulated?
- The dog's medical/behaviour history – has he got any medical conditions? Does he have any allergies? Does he have food-aggression? Is he dog-reactive?
- The dog's likes, dislikes and typical behaviours – what does he like? What does he not like? What makes him scared? What makes him happy? What's normal behaviour for him?

Once we have a thorough understanding of what makes the dog the animal that he is, we can approach things sensitively through a bespoke care plan.

Observing the entire context around us and the dog enables us to make an educated guess as to what is *causing* a dog to be afraid, and then work on building his confidence from that point.

Knowing more about how the dog is feeling makes us more successful in establishing trust, and preventing further emotional and/or physical trauma.

Usually, we can pinpoint the cause fairly quickly just by asking the guardian the right questions and observing the behaviours of the dog in context. Thankfully, most fears can be resolved through counter-conditioning, positive training techniques and time.

Case Study

Grute, the Malamute, was trained by a former owner using a choke collar and correction sprays. This approach worked for a little while, before a tragic event when an infant member of the family yanked his lead and resulted in the dog biting the child.

Grute wasn't reported and was instead sent to a breed specific dog shelter, where he is now awaiting assessment.

One month later, the shelter calls the nearest Holistic Groomer to help with giving him a thorough bath and matt-removal. During that month, Grute has been showing signs of progress, and is almost ready to be put up for adoption.

The groomer asks all the relevant questions to help her devise the groom in advance to suit Grute's individual needs. She decides it would be more stressful to take Grute to yet another unfamiliar environment that may prove to be too stressful, too soon.

She decides that Grute will need a few shorter sessions to work at establishing trust. In these sessions, she plans to introduce sounds, basic handling and objects (including a muzzle) to Grute gradually, using only positive methods.

The first two sessions go amazingly well, and Grute is now ready for a full-body brush out. Due to his bite history, the groomer decides a muzzle is best initially, but decides that a collar and lead might trigger a negative response.

She decides that Grute's shelter handler can help to feed high value liver paste via a wooden spatula through his muzzle whilst being brushed simultaneously. The treat finishes, the brushing stops, they have a break, and then resume until the entire body is thoroughly brushed and matt-free.

Grute wasn't forced into anything negative, and will be more trusting of the groomer going forward.

The goal of a groomer when dealing with a fearful dog is to keep him as calm as possible by adapting a specific approach. Restraints can be a danger to an already fearful dog; especially those with unclear pasts and evident trauma.

The safest defence of a Holistic Groomer will always be observation, as I've already mentioned, like a million times (sorry!).

Preparing a Rescue Dog for Grooming

Remember that the history of a dog that has been rescued will be limited a great deal, and in many circumstances (particularly with rescues from abroad), the handler will never be able to comprehend the level of suffering the dog has been through.

Whether it's neglect, abuse, or simply that the dog has lived on the streets his entire life – the important thing for us all to consider is that it is going to take time, a lot of time.

When I get an enquiry to groom a rescue dog my very first two questions are:

What is the current state of the dog? And,

When did you bring him home?

It can take most dogs up to three months to adapt to his new home environment, and establish some trusting relationships with his new social group. Three months! (Sometimes longer depending on how deep-rooted his trauma is).

In some of the less severe cases, it may take a lot less but the point is it's our responsibility to establish which case we are dealing with before we think about booking the dog in for a grooming session.

When a family has decided to share their home with a dog who has experienced deep trauma, they have to be prepared to work hard. It would be worthwhile to first invest in a positive behaviourist and trainer to help build the dogs confidence to a whole new way of living *before* considering a professional grooming appointment.

The Holistic Groomer could then work alongside the behaviourist to ensure the approach to grooming won't cause any further psychological and/or emotional trauma. Obviously, some groomers (like me) are also Certified Canine Behaviourists and are more than capable of providing an all-in-one service (just remember that they will be more expensive than the average groomer, and rightly so).

In some cases, the cause of the dog's fear is transparent (if a dog has been rescued by the local authority where their living conditions were in total breach of the Animal Welfare Act 2006 – think puppy farms, and general neglect cases), and the professionals will have something to work with straight away.

Either way, rescues will need time to adapt to their new environment, and families so unless it's a welfare case, I would be advising guardians to hold off grooming until the dog is more settled.

Case Study

Rex is a 7-year-old Jack Russell, whose mother (among others) was rescued from a notorious puppy farm that had been operating for many, many years.

Thankfully, Rex was born in the safety of the dog shelter where he was well-cared for.

However, it has been noted from Rex's handlers that he and his only sibling have displayed an extreme fear of crates from a very early age. Rex's parents were born, raised and used in the puppy farm, and it's possible that his grandparents were, too, highlighting that Transgenerational Trauma could be at play.

Rex attends his first grooming appointment, where the groomer witnesses the extent of the dog's phobia. When placed in the holding crate, Rex defecates instantly. He panics and displays some extremely worrying behaviours that the groomer wasn't prepared for.

He's panting, bashing off the crate, salivating, barking and whining.

The groomer is in shock and is afraid to do anything

further with Rex. She immediately calls the guardian to collect.

Rex has never experienced any significant traumatic experience involving a crate that would explain his erratic behaviours, however, the Holistic Groomer will know how history and lineage can explain trauma on a more cellular level.

In this instance, it is more than likely that Rex has Transgenerational Trauma caused by the years of abuse his parents - and possibly grandparents - went through at the puppy farm.

The Holistic Groomer will now know how to adapt their approach to avoid triggering a stress response from Rex in the future, including:

- Remove crates from Rex's view (cover with blankets or keep in a different room).
- Book Rex in as the last dog of the day, and ensure no other dogs are in the premises, to allow him free run of the salon.
- Avoid any potentially restrictive situations that may trigger a response. Pay attention specifically to bathing, and observe Rex's response to things that share the same material, construction or sounds as a crate (restraints clanging off an H-Bar, for example).
- Be prepared to groom Rex on the floor using consent-based methods until trust is established.

These extreme cases are often never resolved, and so, by implementing some of the above adaptations, we are at least managing Rex's specific needs to prevent a trigger, if not resolving them entirely.

Welfare Grooms

I mentioned that one of the first questions I ask a guardian is "what is the current state of the dog", and that's because we need to know whether the dog requires a welfare groom.

So, what is a welfare groom exactly?

In short, a welfare groom basically means that a dog requires urgent grooming attention to prevent suffering.

Example: severe matting that requires a clip-off, parasites, overgrown nails that are puncturing the pads or causing discomfort, a skin infection that needs a medicated bath to maintain etc.

Sadly, it is often impossible for any groomer (holistic or not) to perform a welfare groom without triggering the dog in some way, using an element of force and/or causing some form of emotional/physical trauma.

Not only are welfare grooms strenuous on the dog, but they can also be extremely distressing for the groomer too.

Neglect cases are not uncommon in our industry, and groomers all around the world actively campaign to raise awareness of these problems in an attempt to try and force the welfare authorities to do more in these instances.

There are a few things the Holistic Groomer should consider:

- Is a welfare groom at the groomers the best option for the dog?
- Am I confident and experienced enough to perform the welfare groom safely?
- Do I have the right facilities and tools available to remove matts with ease?
- Does the guardian have realistic expectations of what is possible, and is she aware of the risks in the procedure?

There are many dogs that can cope with a welfare groom within the grooming environment, and of course, we have a duty of care to ensure that we prevent further suffering by proceeding with clip offs, and treatments as and when we are faced with them. However, let's take a closer look at the reality of performing a welfare groom:

- Welfare grooms are complex and physically and mentally exhausting for both the groomer and the dog.
- Welfare cases can conceal severe underlying medical conditions/injuries like skin infections, parasites, open wounds, and sores that might require immediate Veterinary attention.
- Welfare clip-offs can result in unavoidable injuries based on the severity of the matts – cuts, irritated skin, and burns.
- Many shelter dogs have an unclear medical history – high stress can increase the risk of seizures in many cases.
- Many shelter dogs have an unclear behavioural history

– they could have erratic behaviours, a fast-pace escalation of behaviours resulting in an immediate survival response (specifically fight and faint).

- Welfare clip-offs take time, patience and concentration which might not be an option if the dog has deep-rooted trauma.

Therefore, when it comes to *extreme* welfare cases, I always refer to my affiliate Vets for a sedated clip off (health permitting), or request that I perform the clip-off under the supervision of the Vet so that I am confident that the dog is in the best possible hands.

Note: It is far better to refer a case that you know is past your level of expertise than to fake it and potentially risk making matters worse. Similarly, you should never just turn the guardian away with no other option. Always arrange an appointment with the Vet or more experienced groomer yourself, to ensure the dog is getting the attention he requires. And follow up.

When this isn't an option, the last alternative I will consider is performing the welfare groom in the guardian's home with the guardian present.

1. They can help with handling.
2. The dog will most likely feel more relaxed in a familiar environment and be less anxious.
3. The guardian will appreciate the strenuous task it is and be more likely to keep up with maintenance in the future.

The guardian should sign a Welfare Groom Disclaimer to show that they understand the risks involved, which will cover you from any of the above risks should they happen.

Always, always have the Vet on stand-by regardless.

Breed Specific Grooming Woes

As groomers we can always prepare our environment and approach further based on what breed a dog is and their specific genetics, anatomy and physiological needs.

Some dogs are at a physical disadvantage due to bad breeding, which can make the grooming environment a more stressful experience for the dog if we are not careful.

Brachycephalic dogs (such as French Bulldogs) particularly, and those with excessive wrinkles (such as Shar Pei's), require thorough health-checks, and more bespoke grooming rituals during a groom, and here's why:

- Breathing difficulties mean that we must be mindful of a dog's heart rate, avoiding overly stressful situations as well as powerful hair drying tools that could hinder breathing further.
- Excessive wrinkles/folds are a breeding nest for yeast infections, therefore failure to properly cleanse and dry these areas certainly make a dog more vulnerable to infection, disease, pain and/or discomfort.
- "Bug eyes" (common in breeds such as Shih Tzus and Chihuahuas) are easily dislodged from their sockets, so great care must be taken when handling the head;

avoiding any bumps, ensuring our brushing technique is correct, and putting zero pressure on the neck at all.

- Wool coats require the correct bathing and drying technique, along with strenuous brushing and combing, both at home and professionally.

- Mixed wool coats found in all of our Poodle and Bichon mixes are particularly a real problem due to the inconsistency of coat textures.

- Reckless breeding of the same breed - or mixes - may also result in unexpected health and behaviour defects, including exceptionally sensitive skin, or neurological conditions that, sadly, cannot be resolved through training.

- Double Coats are prone to rising damp, when not dried properly which can be a breeding ground for hot spots and yeast infections.

- I've noticed that lighter coated dogs are more sensitive to touch and tend to have problems with skin allergies. Therefore, I would always recommend a lighter hand with your slicker when working with these types of dogs.

9

PREMIUM SERVICES, ETHICAL VALUES & UNWAVERING PRINCIPLES

"My mother told me that the key to success is happiness. My teacher asked me what I wanted to be when I grew up. I said HAPPY. She said that I didn't understand the question. I said that she didn't understand life."

— *JOHN LENNON*

WELL FIRST OF ALL, WHAT DO WE EVEN MEAN WHEN WE CALL something a 'professional' trade?

Writer, Nico Lutkins, wrote that *"being a professional is a state of mind"*, and that she believes it defines *"people who see their working life as a journey to where they are constantly learning and developing."* This was all written in her refreshing article, *'What's the difference between a worker and a professional?'*[1] (By the way, I LOVE this concept)!

But Nico's outlook is still relatively new and, still, a vast majority of people consider professionals to be individuals with a very specialised skill-set, requiring strong academic foundations, coupled with some meaningful ethical standards (Surgeons, Doctors, Lawyers, Teachers, etc).

And with professional status... comes premium pricing!

I've spoken to many groomers over the last few years, and many of them originally came from well-respected professional sectors on high incomes.

The three most common reasons for people leaving 'successful' corporate jobs to work in the grooming industry included:

1. The job wasn't making them happy.
2. They didn't feel like they were making a difference.
3. They were fed up working for someone else, and wanted to do something they could control.

It's clear by the response I got during my research, that success wasn't determined by how much money a person made in a year, but how happy and/or satisfied they were in life in general.

Therefore, statements like, *"You will never make a lot of money"* or *"You will never have financial security"* that are commonly stated by people when referring to Dog Grooming, is irrelevant anyway, because for most of us, it's not about being rich - it's about making a difference to the lives of our beloved animals (corny, but true).

My parents subconsciously taught me a valuable lesson every single day of my childhood:

Working on something you don't love doing will never make you happy, and money isn't everything.

And, if I may add another of their informal teachings…

Doing something you are good at - or trained in - doesn't mean you should do it for a living.

Valuable lessons.

True Story

As a kid, my teachers discovered I was good at music. I enjoyed singing and acting, so naturally, I was encouraged to pursue my gift through theatre. I believed this was my calling, and whilst I enjoyed it for a while, it took me 16 years to realise that it wasn't actually making me happy.

I never landed any main roles because I had terrible stage fright, and would suffer the most horrendous panic attacks prior to performance. I used to spend hours self-loathing because I couldn't understand why I wasn't able to overcome my fear of the spotlight.

After a long while, I realised that being good at something wasn't the same as being in love with something – and that's what many people get wrong when deciding what they want to do for a job or career.

Take Responsibility

You have to be responsible for all that you do. Every decision, every mistake and every lesson learnt – it's all down to you.

My nana used to say, *"Every girl has the exact love life that she wants"*, but it's only now I understand just how wise a statement this is.

If work isn't working for you, then do something about it.

So if holistic grooming is something you LOVE how do we how do we make sure we are doing all we can?

- We invest in our education and we continue to learn for as long as we work.
- We practice what we learn every single day.
- We talk about what we've learnt to everyone - and anyone - who will listen. We prove to the world that we know what we're talking about, and that we are committed to expanding our skill-set long into the future.
- We believe in who we are, what we are worth and why we deserve to be valued as professionals.

If you follow these steps, I guarantee you will attract the most wonderful pet guardians who are more than happy to invest in the best for their beloved animals.

Raising awareness of the value in grooming

Groomers often see a dog in its lifetime just as much - if not more - than their conventional Vet will see them. This means we have so many opportunities to recognise early signs of injury, infection and/or disease.

But do guardians realise this? I mean *really* realise this?

Sure, we can further expand on our abilities by investing in our knowledge in behaviour, and expanding our skill-set to include a range of alternative therapies designed to help the many health conditions we commonly see on a daily basis (with guardian and Vet permission, of course), but what about the rest of it?

What about picking up on sudden changes to the coat texture, skin condition, and even physical stance of the dog? What about discovering a well-conceived cyst, or an abscess in the gum? These are all things that groomers actively highlight to guardians on a daily basis!

Whilst we must be careful never to diagnose as per the VSA, grooming and Holistic Grooming gives us invaluable insight and skills that can help relieve pain and/or potentially save the animal's life. That, my friends, is a service that all doting guardians value more than any Breed Standard trim, I can assure you.

I guarantee that if we spent as much time advertising true grooming as we do styling, then guardians would be queueing up to pay a little bit more for our time and talents.

And the whole world would start to respect us a whole lot more too (I'm in, who else?!).

Drama, Drama, Drama!

I spent the majority of my childhood chasing a dream that I would be the next Audrey Hepburn.

From getting to perform as a prostitute in Les Misérables (not the moment in bright lights I had envisioned, I'll admit), to running numerous events in the pub/club scene as one of Ayrshire's very few female DJs, I know all about entertainment.

But drama is an extremely vain and cut-throat industry. Some might say it's a dog-eat-dog world. How appropriate!

It's definitely not holistic, which is why I chose to leave it behind and work with animals.

Yet sadly, there's a lot about the industry I'm now in that's very similar…

There's a lot of drama queens who have been seduced by the glitz and glam of being the world's 'Next Top Stylist' (no, it's not an actual show…yet!), and whilst I love to fight for my dreams as much as the next Prima Donna, we must remember that dogs aren't objects, projects or accessories. There's so much more to our industry than 'putting on a good show'.

It's great to have ambition and showcase the fun parts about our industry, please don't get me wrong, but does the competition world do a good job at showcasing the real life-changing good groomers do on a daily basis?

Just remember: we aren't shallow, we aren't uneducated, and we aren't merely 'doggy-hairdressers'.

Quite the contrary.

Holistic Grooming hopes to bring our industry's value back to reality, by showing the world what really goes on (at least ideally) behind the scenes.

Note to guardians: don't take the media too seriously. Whilst we all love to be entertained, the majority of television programmes are scripted and/or manipulated in some way (trust me, I know!)

True Story

When I was actively working as a DJ in my younger days, I decided to expand my business into Vocal Coaching, too. In doing quite well at it, I one day received an email advertising a new singing contest show that was looking for applicants to take part, and I immediately registered my interest for the opportunity to raise my brand and get my name out there.

After receiving a visit from the producer, I was assured that my entertainment firm would be well advertised and that the whole thing would be a great publicity opportunity for my business.

The reality, however, was that the entire thing was scripted and very much manipulated for entertainment purposes, and my business wasn't even advertised at all!

What's more, my reputation as a Vocal Coach was truly tainted because the show turned out to be a DATING show. AND I was rejected by a man I didn't even want to date anyway - on national television! (Mortified)!

Grooming is not entertainment, it's real life!

I know I've kinda said it already (here she goes again!) but:

It's time to consider how our industry comes across on television, because being aware of how we come across to the masses really is important when it comes to showing our value.

Lesson: we can be swept away with the idea that putting ourselves out there in the limelight is going to be beneficial to our reputation, when the reality is that it can actually do us a lot more harm than good...

I guess it comes down to this:

If we want to have 'professional status' just like Vets and other pet professionals, we need to show the world that what we do is so much more than just an "art form".

And it's definitely not entertainment.

First and foremost, we are providing a service that safeguards the welfare – the health and wellbeing – of sentient animals. This requires dedication, skill, a sound eye and a lot of patience and love to master.

And don't get me wrong, I know that anthropomorphism[2] isn't always a bad thing! It's good that we consider our animals extensions of our human family, and relate to them as furry children – this only highlights our adoration for them even more, but it's about taking all that we have learned from this book, and others, to make sure that we are not taking our infatuation with dogs to the extreme either.

It's about doing what is *right for the dog* based on *what he needs,* versus *what we would like* the dog to have based on *what we want.*

I'll leave that with you…

10

TOGETHER WE ARE STRONGER

"If everyone is moving forward together then success takes care of itself."

— HENRY FORD

LESSON NUMBER ONE: HOLD BACK JUDGEMENT AND unrealistic expectations![1]

Here's the truth:

1. There's too much judgment (and blame) put on guardians in the grooming world, but Holistic Grooming is about compassion to all and reading between the lines when something at first just doesn't make sense.

2. There are too many guardians (and other pet professionals) out there with unrealistic expectations,

putting unnecessary pressure on the groomer to achieve the perfectly primped dog. But Holistic Grooming is about respecting that each dog is an individual, and that the service of care should not be rushed (or forced).

3. There are too many groomers attacking and judging one another unnecessarily also! Holistic Grooming is about cheerleading for another's success, supporting another's weaknesses, and always being available to provide help and inspiration to a person in need.

Let's begin with the first point, shall we?

Part One – Gaurdian's Perspective

Aside from unrealistic expectations (which we'll talk about in the next section), the most common issue a groomer might have with a guardian is repetitive matting/welfare cases. We hate it, and it's not hard to think of reasons why that is.

Matts particularly are painful on the dog. Matts prevent the dog from regulating his body temperature as he should, and they can also restrict his motion too. They compact and pull the skin taught causing bruising, other nasty skin abrasions and sores too (I've highlighted the horror of matts earlier, refer back for a re-cap if need be).

What's more, by law (the good one that is), a groomer cannot work on removing a matt for more than 15-minutes before it has to be clipped off – the majority of Holistic Groomers don't even attempt to manually remove a matt due to the discomfort it causes.

There is no denying that we see some of the worst animal neglect cases in our line of work, which puts us under an immense amount of emotional strain. Over time, we can become less compassionate towards some guardians who continue to bring in their matted pets.

It's hard – there's no denying that it's hard. We want nothing more than to take a dog home with us if we believe he is suffering. And believe me, there are many dogs that do deserve better.

But it's because of these experiences, there are now many "Blacklist" and "Refuse To Groom" groups circulating designed to warn fellow groomers about guardians who maybe don't pay, continue to bring in matted dogs, and/or share their home with 'Satan's Dog'.

Being a Holistic Groomer however, is about reading between the lines in these instances, before jumping to any, and every conclusion.

We might ask ourselves:

Why does this dog always have matts?
Does the guardian know how to brush correctly?
Do they have the correct tools and/or equipment?
Could I offer to demonstrate to them again?
Why is this dog only at the spa once a year?
Are they struggling for money?

Do they live alone, and rely on others to bring them to the salon?

Sometimes it's not as black and white as the guardian simply doesn't care enough to spend time training and/or brushing their dog (though it does happen, and these cases really do need addressing – yesterday, but today will do).

The truth is we never really know for sure what goes on behind closed doors, therefore it would be wise to think carefully before deciding never to groom a certain dog again...

True Story

*****Caution – this story may cause some distress*****

In 2019 I met a lady and her dog for a meet and treat prior to a grooming appointment. During this consultation, the lady spoke of her experience with Vets in the area and how she had never been able to pay for treatment, and so instead would hop from practice to practice.

I decided I was fully booked for the remainder of the year!

Early in 2020, a local dog owner was prosecuted for animal neglect after her (at that point) unrecognisable dog was found dead in a cardboard box outside. Investigators suspect that part of the cause of death was down to the dog's extensive matting. Animal lovers far and wide expressed their anger on this particular story via social media, including myself.

Fast forward a few weeks, and I received a text one Saturday (my day off) from the lady I had met in 2019, asking for help to remove matting from her dog who was struggling to go to the toilet.

Out of judgment, I said no.

And then immediately, I felt ashamed.

The story of the dead dog from a few weeks earlier flashed into my mind, and suddenly I asked myself how many groomers had turned that owner away out of judgement, or for fear of not getting paid?

I called my lady and told her to meet me at my salon in 15 minutes (so at least still on my terms), where I removed the matting and helped the dog without expecting anything in return.

The lady was clearly grateful after telling me I was the third person she had asked. To my surprise, she paid me, and booked in for a full groom for one month later.

The moral of this story is that judgement can be dangerous, and our decisions could very well play a part in some of the most terrible animal neglect cases we see. Remember, whatever we decide – and why we decide it - it's the animal who has something to gain, or everything to lose.

My experience helped me reconnect with my compassion and empathy, and inspired me to implement a business strategy that allows me to donate my services frequently throughout the year to the cases that need me the most. It's something I'm very proud of both personally and professionally.

Perhaps this is something you could incorporate into yours too?

Educating the Guardian

Spend time getting to know a dog guardian because:

1. They provide you with your livelihood.
2. They want what's best for their dog, and so do you.
3. It can make your job a whole lot easier having them on board.

Working with the guardian will help to ensure that the dog has the best chance of enjoying the grooming experience – and a healthy future - for many years to come.

It's even worthwhile investing in Employers Liability Insurance (if you haven't already) so that you can run masterclasses and workshops specifically to educate them too! If Lockdown 2020 (and 2021) has taught us anything, it's to expect the unexpected! And grooming is one less thing to worry about if you have already taught the guardian how to maintain their dog's coat should we ever have to close our salons for an extended period of time again.

Note: There was a devastating demand for welfare grooming post-lockdown (the first one), and numerous injuries to dogs due to grooming attempts by desperate guardians had ensued. It's important now more than ever to help guardians learn the necessary skills required in maintaining the health and well-being of their dog by themselves.

Remember, I'm not talking about styling – I'm talking about *grooming*.

Be Honest – Be Kind

Equally, it's important to be honest with our dog guardians from the very beginning. We must also be realistic with our capabilities and never bite off more than we can chew!

You might think that showing such transparency is foolish, counter-productive, or even unprofessional but when it comes to dealing with living animals and sharp objects, it's far better to refer on to someone more experienced to allow yourself the time to go out and learn more!

Honesty is a virtue that your clients will come to adore and respect.

Part Two –Groomer's Perspective

The 'Just Get It Done' Mindset

Some pressure a groomer might face will come from unrealistic expectations from the guardian, or the guardians lack of understanding of the Holistic Grooming approach itself.

Someone asked me, "how do you convince guardians of the value in Holistic Grooming?", and it is a VERY good question…

The one thing I will constantly tell guardians is that Holistic Grooming is a life-long journey into health and wellbeing. It is not a "one-off service" – it's a commitment to ensuring their dog is as stress-free as possible in environments that would otherwise be scary to them.

Once the guardian understands the relevance of Holistic Grooming, and how it is part of the jigsaw puzzle that makes the whole dog healthy, and happy, the Holistic Groomer can truly flourish.

I'm talking about:

- Saying goodbye to time-restraints – there is nothing more stressful than feeling pressured to do something in very little time. Charging by the hour and ensuring the guardian is free the whole day of the grooming appointment will allow the groomer to go at the dog's own pace. You won't be any longer than two hours, but it's more about not needing to look at the clock every five minutes.
- Saying goodbye to the expectation of a flawless finish – especially when dealing with a more anxious dog. The guardian's first priority should be to ensure their dog is happy. The second should be whether the dog is clean or not. The cherry on the cake is the style they were totally expecting (you just don't need to hear about it more than once!).
- Saying goodbye to a standard rate – one of the biggest challenges is price. This industry is so versatile and varied that there simply cannot be a box-standard rate for all groomers to adhere to. But guardians get what they pay for – if you are a bespoke service that sacrifices quantity for quality (for example), then you have to charge more. Guardians must be willing to pay for the service they

want without guilt tripping the groomer into lowering her prices.

True Story

Back in 2019, I spent three 30-minute sessions over the course of 2 weeks, dedicating my time working with an anxious GSD called Jed – he was only one year old. My goal was to help him overcome a significant fear of the entire grooming process. As expected, I used those appointments to allow Jed the time to build confidence in the grooming environment through the implementation of positive training methods, lots of praise and high value rewards. Things were progressing steadily, but positively.

But Jed was also displaying anxiety at home when his guardian left for work, and had become destructive. The guardian opted for a crate during the day, but had received complaints from her neighbour regarding his excessive barking. It was obvious this needed to be addressed by an experienced (positive) behaviourist. I advised the guardian of this fact, and she had told me a family friend - a well-known trainer in the area who uses outdated methods – was going to start working with him straight away. Sadly, there was no changing her mind.

By the time Jed returned to me for the next stage in his behaviour modification plan (a couple of weeks later), he was displaying extreme anxiety from the moment he entered the salon. I noticed he was now wearing a slip lead, instead of a harness. When I asked the guardian how he was getting on with the trainer, she replied that his handling tools were changed for "better control", and that she now had a corrector spray when the dog started barking. Additionally, the trainer took him out once a day for training, which the guardian was told would help to settle him throughout the day.

There is no denying that this approach had set Jed's progress with me back significantly.

I asked if she would consider changing trainers to one of my recommended professionals so that I could work with them to devise a better care plan for Jed, to which she refused once more.

At this point I made the difficult decision to ask her to find an alternative groomer, as I simply couldn't cater to her needs without compromising my values.

This is probably one of the most challenging and heart-breaking circumstances a Holistic Groomer will face, but it's important to stay true to your ethics here.

I had two options:

1. I could have continued to do what I could to help relieve the dog of stress within the grooming environment and start from scratch each time (which I *wanted* to do, for the dogs' sake).
2. Or, I could believe in my value, and politely request that the guardian seeks a different groomer due to a conflict of ethics (which I *needed* to do for my own self care).

Update (2021)!

A few months ago, the lady in the above case study called me to apologise. Her dog had bitten the trainer and the friendship subsequently ended. She asked me if I could help, promising she would follow my recommendations. I have arranged to catch up with them once lockdown measures have eased.

Be Honest – Be Kind

I want to take this moment to say that it's absolutely ok to admit to your groomer that you are struggling with the upkeep of your dog at home. The important thing is that you address your apprehensions in the first place. There are many ways a groomer might be able to assist you.

During Lockdown I ran an online support group where I posted regular demonstrations of general coat maintenance, but I also provided Zoom consultations to help others step-by-step.

Anxiety, and mental health disorders can have a negative impact on all aspects of your life, including the responsibility of owning a pet – I know it all too well. Once upon a time, I too struggled to stay motivated and would often feel overwhelmed with my ever-growing list of things to do.

While some people do better with an animal to feel responsible for, others realise it's one more thing to add to their basket. The pressure of daily brushing and the fear of doing something wrong can soon spiral out of control – but, you are not alone!

My friend, Freya has designed an online course for guardians with anxiety who struggle with pet care, which I'm very blessed to have been asked to contribute to. It is a wonderful resource for individuals who might struggle to venture outdoors and require help within safety of their home. You can see Resources for a link to this particular programme.

Ask for help, because it's out there.

Part Three – Synchronised Care

"A Dog Is Like A Jigsaw, and Grooming Is Merely One Piece of the puzzle."

— STEPHANIE ZIKMANN

My mentor and friend, Helen Motteram of Pet Professional Network says, "Together we are stronger", and I couldn't have said it better myself.

If you aren't getting it by now, Holistic Grooming isn't just the practice of grooming itself, but the factors around us that help to provide our animals, their guardians, and ourselves with the very best standard of care.

We really are all connected.

Additionally, we want to be able to provide a service that contributes to the overall health and wellbeing of an animal because it makes all the difference to the very lifespan of the dog, and how he feels throughout the rest of his life.

If you recall the case study with Jed the GSD, having a conflict of interest amongst the many pet professionals we work with can jeopardise the progress and very health of the dog. We need to surround ourselves with like-minded individuals, and that includes guardians too.

It takes a whole community to raise a fur-child. Ok, so I may have adapted this quote to suit, but it's true.

Yet one of the most common arguments I hear *against* Holistic Grooming is that we cannot possibly make a lasting difference to the lives of our animals in just a couple of hours, every couple of months, so why waste our time?

Well, a dog is like a jigsaw (see front cover if you don't believe me), and every little piece is made up of every single individual factor that makes a dog a dog.

Think: Grooming, Diet, Behaviour, Lifestyle, History, Genetics, Experiences and so on. They all have their place, connected to one another to make the whole dog complete.

It is relevant because we are working *holistically*, and what does holistic mean again?

Building A Network

Building a 'whole' network of like-minded professionals will ensure that the animals we care for are given a consistent, synchronised care plan in all aspects of their life.

It might take some time to build a list of businesses and individuals that you trust when you first embark on Holistic Grooming, but the groundwork pays off in spades for many years to come. Your guardians will thank you, too. It really is above and beyond stuff.

It's time to pull out the yellow pages (do they still print those?) and search for your local:

Dog trainers, behaviourists, dog walkers, doggy day-cares, veterinary practices, alternative therapy practitioners, and pet sitters!

Networking From Home

And in case Lockdown is the new 'normal' (Dog, I hope not!), let's look at how we might approach networking from the comfort of our home...

1. Google Search and Facebook Search for positive/force-free events and sign yourself up for them!
2. Get to know the industry experts, send them a message and get chatting!

Meeting like-minded people only requires you to turn up to the *virtual* party, the rest should come as naturally as a sniff to the butt.

You can make amazing friendships and learn from leading specialists from across the globe, through the powers of technology. You no longer need to be rich to attend the most attractive events and conferences – it's time to 'zoom' the night away (literally if you're signing into an overseas event!).

Where To Find Holistic Professionals

Just remember to do your due diligence in researching the individuals and businesses you are interested in collaborating with.

It's always best to make sure that you are establishing a relationship for the right reasons rather than for the sake of it.

In other words, don't be tempted to compromise what you truly believe in just to make friends with people who might take you places.

You need to find people who have your best interests at heart. You can find a list of my recommended organisations, and businesses to help source the best, ethical pet professionals for networking and collaboration opportunities.

A NOTE FROM THE AUTHOR

"Magic's just science that we don't understand yet."

— C. CLARKE

Wow! I can't believe I've actually gone and done it. I'm now a real author, with a real book about some real life-changing stuff. Thank you for investing your time in reading The Magic of Holistic Grooming.

Writing this book has been an emotional and spiritual journey that has developed my own practice in ways I could never have imagined. There have been sleepless nights, stress, tears, and even the occasional tantrum!

But I hope that I have succeeded in inspiring you to think about the bigger picture, and think about what the world looks like through the eyes of your canine.

Holistic Grooming has made me a whole lot more confident in my ability to observe, handle and communicate with dogs, and there's no denying that my businesses have thrived in the last year, proving that it is more than possible to make money in an industry you are passionate about.

I hope you are not too disappointed that I decided not to include a chapter on products and alternative therapies – I know that many of you were expecting and hoping for this. But it was my intention to provide you all with a resource that taps into the areas of Holistic Grooming not yet covered. Why repeat information that is already so perfectly demonstrated in other books (Sue Williamson's and Mary Oquendo's to name but two!).

The Pet Industry in general, is already influenced by some of the most driven, dedicated and compassionate professionals in the world, and I am proud to know many of them. I feel blessed to be given this opportunity to take my place by their side in the mission to regulate our sectors under positive and ethical values.

Our dogs deserve nothing less. And neither do we.

Holistic Grooming *is* magical, and I would love nothing more than to hear how my book has helped to inspire you to implement this approach in your own businesses and in your own lives, living with your dogs.

But until then, I wish you all every success and a furry farewell,

Stephanie x

ABOUT THE AUTHOR

Stephanie Zikmann is an award-winning Holistic Dog Groomer and proud Animal Rights and Mental Health advocate who has taken her industry by storm.

She has appeared in many media outlets across the world, where she has helped to educate groomers and guardians alike on how to enhance the grooming experience for all.

You may have heard her speak in BBC Scotland, Barket Place, Pup Fest 21, The 'Doggy Dojo' Podcast, Whippet Media Podcast and Puppy Post Magazine.

Stephanie is also proud to regularly write for the UK's Top Holistic Dog Magazine, 'Edition Dog'.

In 2019 her business was recognised as one of Scotland's Best Pet Grooming businesses and became the finalist for both 'New Start Business', and 'Best Pet Grooming Business' at Scotland's Business Awards and Ayrshire Chamber of Commerce. Since then, she has been the finalist for many other regional and national awards for both her dog Spa, and as a doting Petpreneur.

The launch of both her online training centre, 'The Holistic Grooming Academy', and 'The Canine Centred Grooming Alliance' (which she co-founded) have been introduced to the industry in hope to inspire, support and educate groomers and guardians on how to implement more positive and updated methods of grooming.

'The Holistic Grooming Diploma' is an accredited self-study course, written by Stephanie, for Grooming Professionals looking to enhance their practical skills in grooming, along with an intimate mentoring programme for start-up grooming businesses.

To find out more, or enrol today you can visit her website on: www.stephaniezikmann.coach – please note, there are limited spaces per year.

At home, Stephanie lives with her husband, Scott along with their two boys, Jack and Joey. They have four dogs of mixed variety. Together, they enjoy watching movies, singing songs and going on mini adventures.

REFERENCES

1. The Philosophy of Holistic Grooming

1. See Resources

2. The Human-Canine Bond

1. Grimm, D., 2021. *Ice age Siberian hunters may have domesticated dogs 23,000 years ago.* [online] Science | AAAS. Available at: <https://www.sciencemag.org/news/2021/01/ice-age-siberian-hunters-may-have-domesticated-dogs-23000-years-ago> [Accessed 2 February 2021]

2. McLeod, S., 2018. *Classical Conditioning.* [online] Simplypsychology.org. Available at: <https://www.simplypsychology.org/classical-conditioning.html> [Accessed 29 November 2020].

3. Bates, M., 2018. *Prehistoric Puppy May Be Earliest Evidence of Pet-Human Bonding.* [online] National Geographic News. Available at: <https://www.nationalgeographic.com/news/2018/02/ancient-pet-puppy-oberkassel-stone-age-dog/> [Accessed 2 February 2021].

4. Yong, E., 2016. *A New Origin Story For Dogs.* [online] The Atlantic. Available at: <https://www.theatlantic.com/science/archive/2016/06/the-origin-of-dogs/484976/> [Accessed 26 January 2021].

5. Geggel, L., 2020. *Stone Age Dog May Have Been Buried With Its Master.* [online] livescience.com. Available at: <https://www.livescience.com/stone-age-dog-burial.html#:~:text=The%20new%20discovery%20is%20hardly,Journal%20of%20Archaeological%20Science%20found.> [Accessed 29 November 2020].

6. Grimm, D., 2017. *These May Be The World's First Images Of Dogs—And They're Wearing Leashes.* [online] Science | AAAS. Available at: <https://www.sciencemag.org/news/2017/11/these-may-be-world-s-first-images-dogs-and-they-re-wearing-leashes> [Accessed 29 November 2020] and https://youtu.be/NAGprHaKAZo

7. Jones, L., 2016. *A Soviet Scientist Created The Only Tame Foxes In The World.* [online] Bbc.co.uk. Available at: <http://www.bbc.co.uk/earth/

story/20160912-a-soviet-scientist-created-the-only-tame-foxes-in-the-world> [Accessed 29 November 2020].

8. Pepper, F., 2019. *The Aussie Who Bred The Labradoodle Says He Created A 'Frankenstein's Monster'.* [online] Abc.net.au. Available at: <https://www.abc.net.au/news/science/2019-09-23/labradoodle-guide-dogs-designer-regret/10717186> [Accessed 19 January 2021].

9. Lane, H., 2017. *Why Do People Buy Dogs With Potential Welfare Problems Related To Extreme Conformation And Inherited Disease? A Representative Study Of Danish Owners Of Four Small Dog Breeds | Dog Breeds.* [online] Pages.wustl.edu. Available at: <https://pages.wustl.edu/dogbreeds/articles/36133> [Accessed 29 November 2020].

10. Dugatkin, L., 2018. *The silver fox domestication experiment.* [online]. Available at: https://evolution-outreach.biomedcentral.com/articles/10.1186/s12052-018-0090-x [Accessed 27 January 2021].

11. Wood, C., 2020. *Covid: Concerns Over 'Dogfishing' And Abandoned Pets.* [online] BBC News. Available at: <https://www.bbc.co.uk/news/uk-wales-54643823> [Accessed 19 January 2021].

3. The History of Grooming

1. Connexion, G., 2021. *Grooming Business Awards Show With Nicky Renwood.* [online] Groomers Connexion. Available at: <https://www.youtube.com/watch?fbclid=IwAR37z6GCEvA_hiDohotTfcpNQNvNwWdFcxthsY02IGDULvF6xGZW1EbZvBM&v=WamLpdajoH8&feature=youtu.be> [Accessed 20 January 2021].

2. Merriam-webster.com. n.d. *Definition Of ALLOGROOM.* [online] Available at: <https://www.merriam-webster.com/dictionary/allogroom> [Accessed 23 January 2021].

3. BBC Earth. 2009. *Monkey Spa.* [online] Available at: <https://www.youtube.com/watch?v=ItWDAoBlEog> [Accessed 23 January 2021].

4. En.wikipedia.org. 2020. *Comfort Behaviour In Animals.* [online] Available at: <https://en.wikipedia.org/wiki/Comfort_behaviour_in_animals> [Accessed 26 November 2020].

5. Engel, C., 2003. *Wild Health.* London: Phoenix.

6. Shelbourne, T., 2012. *The Truth About Wolves & Dogs.* Dorchester: Hubble & Hattie.

7. Goodall, J. and Berman, P., 2014. *Reason for Hope.* New York: Grand Central Publishing.

8. Conditional Allo-Grooming Report on Wood Mice. Accessed: 26

November 2020. https://academic.oup.com/beheco/article/12/5/584/311685

9. Liu, D., 1997. Maternal Care, Hippocampal Glucocorticoid Receptors, and Hypothalamic-Pituitary-Adrenal Responses to Stress. *Science*, 277(5332), pp.1659-1662.

10. Peres, C., 1996. [online] Available at: <https://www.jstor.org/stable/4163652?seq=1> [Accessed 26 November 2020].

11. Tsang, J., 2018. *Should You Let Your Dog Lick Your Face?*. [online] Massivesci.com. Available at: <https://massivesci.com/articles/dog-lick-face-healthy-safe/#:~:text=In a recent analysis of, holes in bacterial cell membranes> [Accessed 26 November 2020].

12. Engel, C., 2003. *Wild Health*. London: Phoenix.

13. Mark, J., 2017. *Dogs In Ancient Egypt*. [online] Ancient History Encyclopedia. Available at: <https://www.ancient.eu/article/1031/dogs-in-ancient-egypt/> [Accessed 26 November 2020].

14. Labradaor and Beagle Saliva Experiments: https://www.ncbi.nlm.nih.gov/pmc/articles/PMC5969230/

15. Wilhelm, F. H., Kochar, A. S., Roth, W. T., & Gross, J. J. (2001). Social anxiety and response to touch: Incongruence between self-evaluative and physiological reactions. Biological Psychology, 58, 181-202

16. Ogle, M., 1997. *From Problems To Profits*. Sonora, Calif.: Madson Group.

17. Frankroweandson.com. 2019. *History Of Grooming*. [online] Available at: <https://www.frankroweandson.com/blog/post/history-of-grooming/> [Accessed 26 November 2020].

4. The Grooming Industry

1. Gladwell, A., 2018. *Extreme Dog Grooming: Harmless Fun Or Threat To Pets?*. [online] BBC News. Available at: <https://www.bbc.co.uk/news/uk-england-43416967> [Accessed 23 January 2021].

5. Legislation and The Law

1. Parliament.scot. 2018. *Call For Evidence - Control Of Dogs (Scotland) Act 2010*. [online] Available at: <https://www.parliament.scot/S5_Public_Audit/General%20Documents/Control_of_Dogs_Summ_of_Evidence_-_SPICe_Oct_2018.pdf> [Accessed 19 January 2021].

2. Mellor DJ & Reid CSW (1994) Concepts of animal well-being and predicting the impact of procedures on experimental animals. In Improving the Well-Being of Animals in the Research Environment; Australian and New Zealand Council for the Care of Animals in Research and Teaching (ANZCCART): Glen Osmond, SA, Australia, pp. 3–18.
3. Mellor DJ (2017) Operational details of the Five Domains Models and its key applications to the assessment and management of animal welfare.
4. Mellor DJ & Beausoleil NJ (2015) Extending the 'Five Domains' model for animal welfare assessment to incorporate positive welfare states. Animal Welfare 24:241–253. doi: 10.7120/09627286.24.3.241.
5. Dogstrust.org.uk. 2019. *Stray Dog Survey Report 2018-19 | Dogs Trust.* [online] Available at: <https://www.dogstrust.org.uk/about-us/publications/stray-dog-survey-report-2019> [Accessed 28 December 2020].

6. The Science of Emotions and Behaviour

1. Fishburn, I., 2018. *Kachina Wellness - Kachina.* [online] Kachina. Available at: <https://kachinacanine.com/complete-wellness/> [Accessed 22 December 2020].
2. Kim, D. and Hill, D., 2012. *Emotions Are Energy : The Bodymind Connection And E-Motion.* [online] Authenticity Associates. Available at: <https://www.authenticityassociates.com/emotions-are-energy/#:~:text=What we think of as, literally means energy in motion.> [Accessed 23 January 2021].
3. Carey, B., 2018. *Can We Really Inherit Trauma? (Published 2018).* [online] Nytimes.com. Available at: <https://www.nytimes.com/2018/12/10/health/mind-epigenetics-genes.html#:~:text=The findings C the authors concluded,the gene B there's no mutation.> [Accessed 22 December 2020].
4. Keim, B., 2014. *Brain Scans Show Striking Similarities Between Dogs And Humans.* [online] Wired. Available at: <https://www.wired.com/2014/02/dog-brains-vocal-processing/> [Accessed 29 November 2020].
5. Dr. Group's Healthy Living Articles. n.d. *Environmental Stress: How It Affects Your Health.* [online] Available at: <https://globalhealing.com/natural-health/what-is-environmental-stress/> [Accessed 16 December 2020].
6. Vinopal, L., 2018. *5 Things That Happen When You Bottle Up Your Emotions.* [online] Fatherly. Available at: <https://www.fatherly.com/health-science/health-risks-holding-back-emotions/> [Accessed 30 November 2020].

7. Rugaas, T., 2006. *On Talking Terms With Dogs*. 2nd ed. USA: Dogwise Publishing.

8. Fear Free Pets. 2020. *What Is Fear Free & Why Is It Important? | Fear Free Pets*. [online] Available at: <https://fearfreepets.com/about/what-is-fear-free/> [Accessed 16 December 2020].

9. Fear Free Pets. 2020. *What Is Fear Free & Why Is It Important? | Fear Free Pets*. [online] Available at: <https://fearfreepets.com/about/what-is-fear-free/> [Accessed 16 December 2020].

10. Blake, S., 2016. *Third Eye Chakra; The Psychic Chakra · Earth And Water*. [online] Earth and Water. Available at: <https://earthandwater.co/third-eye-chakra/> [Accessed 4 December 2020].

7. It Starts With 'Self'

1. Cherry, K., 2020. *Why Our Brains Are Hardwired To Focus On The Negative*. [online] Verywell Mind. Available at: <https://www.verywellmind.com/negative-bias-4589618> [Accessed 23 January 2021].
   Doon, M., 2008. *Interview With Dr. Masaru Emoto*.

2. Doon, M., 2008. *Interview With Dr. Masaru Emoto*. [online] YouTube. Available at: <https://www.youtube.com/watch?v=ujQAk9EM3xg> [Accessed 23 January 2021].

3. La Porte, D., 2019. *Words Can Make You Sick. Or Healed. Heavy Or Light. Here'S An Experiment That Might Prove It.*. [online] Medium. Available at: <https://daniellelaporte.medium.com/words-can-make-you-sick-or-healed-heavy-or-light-heres-an-experiment-that-might-prove-it-db115022c82f>

4. Cousins, L., 2018. *Why 'Bottling It Up' Can Be Harmful To Your Health | HCF*. [online] Hcf.com.au. Available at: <https://www.hcf.com.au/health-agenda/body-mind/mental-health/downsides-to-always-being-positive> [Accessed 23 January 2021].

5. Mayoclinic.org. 2019. *About Mayo Clinic - About Us - Mayo Clinic*. [online] Available at: <https://www.mayoclinic.org/about-mayo-clinic> [Accessed 15 December 2020].

6. Mayoclinic.org. 2019. *About Mayo Clinic - About Us - Mayo Clinic*. [online] Available at: <https://www.mayoclinic.org/about-mayo-clinic> [Accessed 15 December 2020].

7. Griebel, M., n.d. *5 Benefits Of Stretching | Preferred Physical Therapy*. [online] Preferred Physical Therapy. Available at: <https://www.preferredptkc.com/5-benefits-of-stretching/>

8. nhs.uk. 2021. *Why Lack Of Sleep Is Bad For Your Health*. [online] Avail-

able at: <https://www.nhs.uk/live-well/sleep-and-tiredness/why-lack-of-sleep-is-bad-for-your-health/> [Accessed 19 January 2021].

9. Brené Brown, research professor, University of Houston and author of "Dare to Lead".

10. *James Maskalyk & Dave Courchene.*

11. Denworth, L., 2019. *How Much Time In Nature Is Needed To See Benefits?.* [online] Psychology Today. Available at: <https://www.psychologytoday.com/us/blog/brain-waves/201906/how-much-time-in-nature-is-needed-see-benefits#:< [Accessed 19 January 2021].

8. The Holistic Grooming Protocol

1. Lloyd J. (2017). Minimising Stress for Patients in the Veterinary Hospital: Why It Is Important and What Can Be Done about It. *Veterinary sciences,* 4(2), 22. https://doi.org/10.3390/vetsci4020022

9. Premium Services, Ethical Values & Unwavering Principles

1. Lutkins, N., 2016. *The Difference Between A Worker and A Professional – And Why It Matters.* [online] Business.linkedin.com. Available at: <https://business.linkedin.com/en-uk/marketing-solutions/blog/posts/adweek-europe/2016/The-difference-between-a-worker-and-a-professional-and-why-it-matters> [Accessed 19 October 2020].

2. Bekoff, M., 2019. *Anthropomorphism Favors Coexistence, Not Deadly Domination.* [online] Psychology Today. Available at: <https://www.psychologytoday.com/us/blog/animal-emotions/201912/anthropomorphism-favors-coexistence-not-deadly-domination> [Accessed 18 January 2021].

10. Together We Are Stronger

1. See Resources

RESOURCES

Further Education and Support for Professionals

Accredited, The Holistic Grooming Diploma and Mentorship Programme – spaces are limited to 10 students every quarter, with a maximum of 40 students per year. To enrol visit: www.stephaniezikmann.coach.

Holistic Dog Grooming for Groomers – free support group for groomers. Visit https://www.facebook.com/groups/holisticgroomingforgroomers.

DAATA Certification Level 1 Course – course on dermatology for dogs, visit: http://fr.daatacertification.com/product-page/lvl-1-special-discount-sz (Code: HolisticQueen).

Zoopharmacognosy with Caroline Ingraham – for a range of amazing courses, visit http://www.carolineingraham.com.

Taking The Grrrr Out of Grooming in the Salon (book) – Sue Williamson.

Publicity for Pet Businesses with Rachel Spencer – visit http://www.publicityforpetbusinesses.co.uk.

Holistic Pet Grooming (book) - by Mary Oquendo and Daryl Connor.

Physiotherapy Webinars with Rachel Jackson – visit http://www.wellbalancedanimals-vetphysio.co.uk.

Further Education and Support for Guardians

Locke's Dogs – Behaviourist & Trainer, Fun Not Fear® – visit http://www.lockesdogs.co.uk.

Holistic Grooming with Stephanie Zikmann – visit https://www.facebook.com/groups/holisticdoggroomingwithstephaniezikmann.

Taking The Grrrr Out of Grooming (book) – Sue Williamson.

Dog Furiendly with Adele Pember – visit http://www.dogfuriendly.com.

'Doggy Dojo' Podcast with Susan Light – visit https://podcasts.apple.com/gb/podcast/doggy-dojo/id1542560229.

Joanne Jarvis – Animal Communication Facilitator, Angelic Reiki Practitioner and Author of Dexter's Diary. Visit: http://www.jjangels.co.uk

Pup Talk with Niki French – for amazing dog training tips, visit: http://www.pup-talk.mykajabi.com/the-pack

Further Education for both Professionals & Guardians

Canine Wellness Course with Dr. Isla Fishburn – 20% off via this link: http://coursecraft.net/courses/z9V7z/a/ cpmYFEt8Q (Code: KACHINA).

Let Animals Lead™ Reiki with Animal Reiki Scotland – for 20% off Level 1 and 2 e-mail alison@ animalreikiscotland.co.uk and quote "The Holistic Dog Groomer". Additionally, a further 10% off all other workshops offered on their website!

Low Stress Handling™ Certification – visit http://www. lowstresshandling.com.

Fear Free™ Certification – visit http://www. fearfreepets.com.

Canine Flow with Caroline Griffiths – visit http://www. canineflow.com.

Tellington Touch – visit http://www.ttouchtraining.co.uk.

International School of Canine Psychology – visit http://www.theiscp.com.

Vita Canis Aromatherapy EBook – 20% off via this link: https://vitacanis.co.uk/product/aromatherapy-for-dog-groomers/ (Code: AROMABOOK).

Barket Place with Caroline Wilkinson – visit http://www.barketplace.uk.

Edition Dog Magazine Subscription – visit http://www.editiondog.com.

WAG (book) – by Zazie Todd

On Talking Terms with Dogs (book) – by Turid Rugaas.

Animals In Translation (book) – by Temple Grandin.

Survival of the Friendliest – by Vanessa Woods and Brian Hare.

Rising Strong – by Brené Brown.

The Emotional Lives of Animals – by Mark Bekoff.

Recommended Organisations

Pet Professional Network – visit http://www.petpronetwork.com

Canine Centred Grooming Alliance – visit http://www.ccgroomingalliance.com.

Holistic Pet Directory – visit http://www.holisticpetdirectory.com.

Welfare for Animals – visit http://www.welfare4animals.org.

Dog Welfare Alliance – visit http://www.thedogwelfarealliance.co.uk.

ICAN – visit http://www.companionanimal.network

INTOdogs – visit http://www.intodogs.org.

UK Dog Behaviour and Training Charter – visit http://www.ukdogcharter.org.

Pet Professional Guild – visit http://www.petprofessionalguild.com.

EPIGRAPH

"You can spend your entire life peeking through the keyhole, trying desperately to see the bigger picture, or you can take a step back and simply open the door..."

— STEPHANIE ZIKMANN

Printed in Great Britain
by Amazon